THE PRAYER

THE PRAYER

68 Words that Changed the World

Christopher Levan

CASCADE *Books* · Eugene, Oregon

THE PRAYER
68 Words that Changed the World

Cascade Books
An Imprint of Wipf and Stock Publishers
199 W. 8th Ave., Suite 3
Eugene, OR 97401

www.wipfandstock.com

PAPERBACK ISBN: 978-1-5326-1815-4
HARDCOVER ISBN: 978-1-4982-4347-6
EBOOK ISBN: 978-1-4982-4346-9

Cataloguing-in-Publication data:

Names: Levan, Christopher.
Title: The Prayer : 68 words that changed the world / Christopher Levan.
Description: Eugene, OR: Cascade Books, 2018 | Includes bibliographical references.
Identifiers: ISBN 978-1-5326-1815-4 (paperback) | ISBN 978-1-4982-4347-6 (hardcover) | ISBN 978-1-4982-4346-9 (ebook)
Subjects: LCSH: Lord's prayer—Meditations.
Classification: BV230 .L40 2018 (print) | BV230 (ebook)

Manufactured in the U.S.A.   SEPTEMBER 11, 2018

Dedicated to two mentors:
John Douglas Hall
John Dominic Crossan

Table of Contents

A Prayer-Full Preface: The Power of Words

LET ME BEGIN WITH a confession. I don't pray. Not in the conventional sense.

If this is true (and it is), it can hardly be a stirring recommendation for a book featuring what has become the most influential prayer in human history. Can an author who doesn't pray have anything worthwhile to say on the subject of the Lord's Prayer?

You might be tempted to reach for the next book on your night table, but stay with me for a few paragraphs, and I will try to point out why the absence of a prayer life is not a disadvantage to those who ask, as the disciples of Jesus did, "Teach us to pray."

We all suffer from misconceptions. For some time, I lived with the misguided impression that really spiritual people are down-on-their-knees praying people. I thought that the superstars of the faith wore patches in the carpet by their beds. "Pray without ceasing." That's what it meant to believe.

No longer. After fifty years of journeying in this Christian way, I can now claim my space as a practicing Christian who doesn't have a prayer life. It no longer troubles me to admit that.

Are you like me? Read on, then.

Of course, it goes without saying that, as a minister, I am a professional "pray-er." That's my job! In the church sanctuary or civic podium, I am called on to "offer a little word of prayer." And I am honored to do that, but I have no illusions. What I say, and what most people would recognize as prayer, is not central to what I consider to be the chief occupation of a Christian.

To be blunt, most of what passes for prayer in our North American world is either public emoting that should remain private or mediocre "spiritual window-shopping" that is far too obviously self-absorbed. In some instances, prayer is like a pistol held to the head of the presumed backsliding sinner—designed to straighten out their misguided thoughts or actions. In a subtler form, I have experienced prayer as an argument clincher. I can't be convinced in an open debate, and so you resort to prayer to have the final word. As a tool of coercion, prayer becomes both punitive and pointless.

I have no need of any of these kinds of prayer: whether as wish list, sloppy sentimentality, or covert manipulation. Neither do you!

Real prayer, the kind that moves mountains and changes the world, is of a different order from what is widely served up as soul food. Authentic prayer is a lifelong conversation with a mystery, a source of strength, and an anchor in the sea changes of life. It's not the actual phrases that are important. The earnest and prayer filled recognize that their words, gestures, or thoughts (all of which might be called prayer) are merely vehicles for a deeper communion. It is through prayer that we touch creation and Creator, and often in ways that we cannot understand, and in a reciprocal manner, we too are touched and transformed. We commune with the universe, so that the universe we make for ourselves is life-giving and just.

I have no illusions. During worship or at public ceremonies, my prayers set a tone. Nothing more. They add reverence and sobriety. I'm not being modest or cynical, aiming too low so as to appear saintly. I do not put much stock in my abilities as a "pray-ee." It is God who is the prayer.

Prayer in many senses is God's work. We speak in prayer, and by uttering words we kick start an ancient conversation in which the Source of All is stirred, moves in us, and through us. At those times when the Spirit is active, prayer becomes a lively dialogue, helping us focus God's will for our lives and this planet.

When this dialogue happens, prayer is real. This genuine prayer has both a corporate and an individual feel and function. In its corporate dimension, prayer establishes an atmosphere of the sacred within this world which God loves, and lends direction to God's movements in the "here and now"—God's mission comes alive. Privately, individual prayer acts as a safe haven, an intimate space where the secrets we cannot share out loud are exchanged.

Alas, this kind of praying, whether private or public, is not a daily feature of my religious life and certainly not something that preoccupies much of my time as a disciple of Jesus or a minister of religion.

Please hear me correctly. I do not pray because I think it is inconsequential or unimportant.

I don't pray because it is so demanding.

People who have the gift of prayer are to be coveted and nurtured. They can accomplish what many disciples either don't have the time or skill to achieve.

However, having confessed that I don't have a prayer life, it does not follow that I am at a loss when it comes to communing with my Creator. In fact, I consider that I have a close relationship with my Maker. We've just never had much to debate. There's no painful push and pull; no break in our unspoken conversation. No fist-shaking at heaven! Why do I need to stop doing what I believe is important or necessary or life-giving or prophetic in order to tell my God what's happening? Surely this is superfluous.

If God is who we say, then God will know what I might need, dream, say or do, long before I think it. I do not need to speak words in order to be praying. In many ways, my reading and writing, communing and constructing, justice-making and peacekeeping are all acts of prayer. As I seek to understand and live the truth, am I not working in concert with my Maker who made me to love and restore the earth? In this sense, the motives and actions that seek to embody God's love and justice are the fullest form of prayer.

In this sense, I consider my life to very prayer-full. How about you? *The Prayer* has been called the "greatest" prayer (Crossan), and while I agree that it is a terribly important prayer that has changed human history, I will argue in this book that it began much more as an enacted and embodying vision than a recital of words.

The Power of Words

However, before we get to the subject in question, let us agree that words have power. In an electronic age, when writing and disseminating words come so easily, the public has lost its appreciation of how the spoken word can change everything. In times past, words had the power to win battles:

> Four score and seven years ago[,] our fathers brought forth on this continent, a new nation, conceived in Liberty, and dedicated to the proposition that all men are created equal. (Abraham Lincoln, "The Gettysburg Address")

Spoken forcefully, words have the capacity to embolden half the human race:

> Women are going to form a chain, a greater sisterhood than the world has ever known. Never explain, never retract, never apologize. Just get the thing done and let them howl. (Nellie McClung)

There are moments, rare but real, when words capture the dreams of an entire race and make the difference between servitude and salvation:

> "I have a dream . . ." (Martin Luther King Jr.)

In all of these examples, there is no magic at work. It's not as if spoken collections of syllables have a supernatural power. On their own, words are nothing more than the production of physiological mechanics and mental dynamics. The power of words rests with the people who grant them influence and importance. If there is magic at work at all it is in the unspoken and yet widely held belief that certain words are to be elevated above others; that some speeches contain such a capsulated form of ultimate truth that they must be seen as another order of human utterance: definitive, sacred, and actionable.

This text argues that the power of words did not begin with the modern age. On the contrary, in times past, words had greater power to change and transform reality than currently. In the first century, for instance, there were many instances when words had the capacity literally to change reality: in judicial and religious settings, for instance. The thesis of this text is that the Prayer is one remarkable, and perhaps the most significant, example in human history, of how words have agency and power. When the followers of Jesus spoke this prayer, they accepted that they were changing their own reality in tangible, binding, and concrete ways.

The Prayer: not to be spoken lightly!

Acknowledgments

A BOOK ON PRAYER, on the Lord's Prayer, to be specific! It's new territory for me. To whom do I owe my inspiration? The author of that great prayer no doubt. But more, I also want to acknowledge Douglas John Hall. It was when I read his book, *When You Pray*, that I found a way to speak of prayer that did not include kneeling pads or daily devotionals—two things I have studiously avoided as a Christian. I owe Doug a great deal for that very reason. He helped me to see prayer as a legitimate mental activity as well as a craft of the heart.

Likewise, when I picked up John Dominic Crossan's text, *Excavating Jesus*, I became convinced that I had been living under a misconception. Prayer, in the traditional sense, is not an essential Christian attribute. Of course, it's restorative and instructive, but if you do not pray in a conventional manner, you're not a heretic. More assurance. His more recent work, *The Greatest Prayer*—while not directly related to this text—is in many ways a work in concert with my own.

Moreover, Crossan helped me to see that the prayer that holds center stage in the Christian ritual cycle, "the Lord's Prayer," may suffer from a serious misunderstanding. It is entirely possible that we have taken it out of its theological and social matrix and domesticated it. Religious mediocrity or cowardice has rubbed off the sharp political edges of the prayer and undermined its social imperatives. It is in the light of Crossan's suggestions that I am writing this text, and I am very grateful for his wisdom.

A further word of gratitude:

African folk wisdom tells us it takes an entire village to raise a child, and the same is true of a book. Consequently, I would like to acknowledge two communities who have helped me. First, the Synod School of the Synod of Lakes and Prairies of the Presbyterian Church USA. We meet each summer in Iowa, and it was among my friends at Synod School that this book was first begun. I am grateful to that circle: Richard Buller, Karen Rae, Tim and Sandy Maxa, Mark Davis, Carol Farrell, Carol Gilson, Burns Stanfield, and Diana Barber. Secondly, it has been the community of Wilmot United Church who have been so helpful and encouraging as I wrote this book. It was in debate with them that I shaped the ideas that are contained here. A special thanks to Bob Breen, Kitty Elton, Jocelyn Howatt, Ted Colson, Lynn Chaplin, Owen Washburn, Cameron Gunn, Bob Jones, Peter Short, Lois Campion, Cheryl Smith, Ian Graham, Greg Black, Garth and Lucille Caseley, Marjorie Atkinson, Priscilla Giestefer, Karen and Phil Smith, Stephen Smith, Murray MacFarlane, Lois MacDougall, and so many more. For your care and comfort, I am grateful.

Then there is my family in Cuba. I couldn't have completed this text without the rejoicing, guidance, and inspiration of Orestes and Wanda, Dora, Ary, and Beidy, Moraima, Justo, Reinerio, Patricia, Chuchi, Monica, and Mateo. It was while enjoying their friendship that the thesis of this book was lived out.

And for the special grace to write, I must thank Ellen, my wife.

I trust this text will be a blessing.

La Habana, Cuba, June 2016
Christopher Levan

Introduction:
Standing in the Need of Prayer

WHEN I WAS TEN, I went to church camp. I thought everyone did. Ryerson Beach Camp. Even now, forty years hence, the very name conjures up vague memories of devotion and delight.

Church camp, a rare beast in these days of "designer children" and high-maintenance summer recreation. At church camp, we had "Vespers." Do you recall Vespers? Any self-respecting twenty-first–century camp would not be caught dead with "Vespers" on its daily agenda of camp activities.

Vespers is a solemn time, a moment of Sabbath to close off the busy day. Seemingly very late at night—though it was probably no more than eight o'clock in the evening—we would wrap ourselves in our blankets and make our way up to a glade in the woods. Split-rail benches in a circle, a table in the center. As the evening shadows grew longer, the director would lead us in a sing-song. My favorite was "Standing in the Need of Prayer." Perhaps you know it? The title gives away most of the plot.

"Not my brother, not my sister, but it's me, oh Lord, standing in the need or prayer."

It has a lively melodic line, but at the time, I had no idea what the lyrics might mean, since I had no real notion of prayer as being an essential part of my life. I'd look around the circle of boys my age, all singing their hearts out about their need for prayer, and wondered if I was the only one who was clueless and didn't pray—no matter how much he "needed" it.

How often now do I meet veterans of church camp who ask about prayer, wanting to know what it means and how it works? They stop me at the back of church, sheepishly fiddle with coat buttons or look at the ceiling tiles and then confess that they "don't pray much" and wonder what it is "all about anyway." It is in response to my own journey of faith and to help others in theirs that I have taken up the subject of praying.

My own doubts notwithstanding, it seems evident that most human beings are standing in the need of prayer. I have watched as cohorts of believers have filed in and out of church buildings, with the title of my childhood song in their hearts "needing prayer." Perhaps it is one of the few common denominators that cross generational and cultural divides. *Homo sapiens* has had a rich spiritual heritage, and the ever-recurring practice of prayer is testimony to our universal desire to communicate with the One (or Ones) who exist beyond the horizon.

Now, if you picked up this book because you know yourself to be someone "standing in the need of prayer," I congratulate you, but you may be initially disappointed. If you've cracked open the first few pages expecting to get a quick spiritual fix with a selection of soul-soothing verses to restore your worn-out heart, something to display on your office cubicle wall or put up as the background to your computer screen, then I suggest you put this text aside and carry on down the shelf. We'll do a good deal of thinking before we get to any practical praying. We're going to focus on *The Prayer,* and as you will see, the correctives I suggest in our understanding of this central Christian prayer tend to be more of a political than a personal nature. However, for those who seek assistance for their prayer life, there is an appendix of prayers for your use. Mind you, they are all versions of the Lord's Prayer, but you will see that it gets translated endlessly over time and place.

Again, let me be clear. If you want help with your spiritual life, I commend you. It's not that I hold such a goal in low esteem. On the contrary, I regard spiritual well-being as a very crucial factor in the life of a believer. As you will see, it is not in the traditional sense that I commit myself to what I would say is "praying the household of God into life."

All my cautions aside, in the Christian North American world, there is no more obvious an indicator of the centrality of prayer as a human activity than the Prayer. It is still commonplace that the mere mention of the first two words of that prayer invokes an immediate response. Say, "Our Father," and the devout will immediately join in to recite the other verses, an ancient list of petitions.

So, I take it as a given that we are all standing in the need of prayer. But I will argue in this text that the prayer that we are needing is *not* the one we are expecting. We do not require another ticket into heaven, a spiritual ladder for our souls to climb out of the grime and grit of daily living. The Prayer that we all know as the "Lord's" was focused on things down here, on earth. There's no disputing the fact that whatever the prayer did for life in heaven, these sixty-eight words changed human history forever.

Prayer as Church Building

This is a book for those who want to understand and deepen their primal need of faith to know the heart of God and how it beats through their lives and their time and place. Our questions: Why do we pray and what do we get out of it? Where does it take us, and how will we know when we get there?

I also explore the question of prayer because it influences how we move forward to rebuild the household of God. By any measure, sociological or theological, the Christian church within this northern new world context is in trouble. Numbers are down and scandals are up. Young people stay away as a matter of principle, and the average age of most historical churches creeps well past retirement. The once politically influential institution that swayed the opinions of presidents and prime ministers is either the voice of radical conservatism or an irrelevant joke.

So far, this is nothing new. Most northern Christians, if they are willing to be sincere and open, know that the project of Christendom—a time when Christianity converted the entire world and its social order—is a failed and flawed dream. It simply ain't going to happen. The crowing of conservative Christian denominations and right-wing political think tanks notwithstanding, the triumphant church is dying. Douglas Hall has been predicting this decline for decades and puts it best when he argues that our church is suffering through a serious "humiliation." We are not what we once were, and our dominant reaction is shame: how did we let the church down?

As a professional in what looks like a losing and increasingly pitiful cause, I am naturally distressed, feeling that the decline of my particular community of faith is my fault. However, it's not the loss of size or status that is distressing, though these things bring understandable levels of grief. It saddens me to see empty and forgotten buildings, once the homes of the devout and the sacred places where we shared one another's burdens, now relegated to architectural dustbins. Frankly, I can live without buildings if necessary, and I realize that the company of Jesus has always experienced an ebb and flow of its social or political importance. What irks me is the mediocrity of our vision. We use our best energy wringing our hands over diving membership rolls, and the best we can muster is either a stoic fatalism about our future or a faddish capitulation to modern marketeering. Survival is the only language we speak now. We hunker down in the faint hope of a last-minute reprieve when our social importance will be restored: when we regain the public high ground and the crowds return. In the cellar of despair, we just keep doing what we've always done, hoping God will send us a different result—the definition of insanity if ever there was one!

In psychological terms, our reaction to our decline looks like either avoidance or suppression.

But let us be honest. It is the poverty of our belief and the shallowness of our mission that renders us irrelevant in the eyes of our fellow citizens. The church is not dying because what we say and do is so controversial, but precisely because it is *not*.

Despite that, I believe we need not lament. Like too much bad theology, the household of God has wasted its best energies exploring what we are not. Why do we not speak of who we are? It is to put just such a positive program for believers in place that I offer this work.

The kingdom movement that Jesus began is not dead. Too often we confuse it with the church, as if the fate of Jesus' mission is inextricably bound up in that of the Christian church. What if we went back and asked again what our founder meant for us to do? Was it to build a church? Is the current structure congruent with the mission of the early Jesus circles? Is it possible that we got it wrong?

It is the thesis of this book that, in fact, we did get sidetracked and that a close reading of the Prayer holds a clue to our mistake and our recovery. If we explore more deeply the implications of this first-century prayer, will we be able to build a vital mission of the disciples of Jesus in twenty-first century? Moreover, I offer the subtitle in a very serious way: *68 Words that Changed the World.* The Prayer is not just a collection of intellectual ideals or a list of spiritual virtues. It is not eloquent poetry. It is an agent of change, like sugar in coffee or salt in bread. The Prayer makes a real, material difference.

The problem for many liberal Christians is that we have ceased to believe the Prayer and thus we do not see its power for transformation.

The key question to ask is the one I raised for myself back at church camp. If we are all "standing in the need of prayer," what does it mean?

What are we actually doing when we begin the most ancient of prayers and speak to God like a "Father"? Do you know?

Would you be surprised if I argued that for at least 1800 years Christians have mistaken the real purpose of the Prayer?

Knowing What We Pray

Another childhood memory.

When I was child I knew the letter in the alphabet that came after "k." It was "elemenohpee." Now truth be told, as a letter, I had never seen "elemenohpee" used in a book or on the chalk board. The teacher didn't write it in my scribbler, ever. But it was there. I knew this because, when we sang the little jingle that helped all elementary students with their ABC's, there it was. Right after "k," "elemenohpee." We'd run through the first eleven letters and then slide over the next one: "elemenohpee."

Grade one misconceptions are hard to break, and it wasn't until the latter part of grade two that I realized my error. Not one letter, but five were described by "elemenohpee." You have to separate them out in order to understand the alphabet. A simple mistake, but for over a year as I recited my ABCs, the teacher heard one thing and I understood another.

Is this what has happened to the Prayer in Christian communities today? We recite it every Sunday, without thinking. It slides off our tongues with very little effort, and we tell ourselves that we know what it means. We have all the words in the right order, but we rarely stop long enough to examine what the actual petitions might have meant when they were uttered by the first audience. Do we give a second glance to the question of what they might mean for our own communities of faith now? The Prayer comes and goes with such speed and regularity that we hardly give it more than a passing consideration. It's what Christians do. It sets a tone of piety, marks us as Christian.

Okay, I can feel you drifting off. Have you yawned yet? Gotten up for a little snack? When I preach, I can tell by the eyes of those who listen whether I have their attention, whether what I am saying makes sense, but these pages separate us. I can't tell how well you are listening. So, let me try a more direct conversation.

"Do you ever think about what you are actually praying?"
You look quizzical. "Is that a trick question?"

"I think prayer can actually change us."

"Am I missing something?" you ask.

"There might be more," I reply.

"Oh." Your eyes are glazing over. "But it's a big enough effort just to get to a church pew at all."

"True." I'll admit it. "Given the crimped and crammed lifestyles we lead, it's a wonder we achieve that much. But what if prayer could be more? So much more."

"I'm listening," you say. "But asking for a coherent interpretation of a centuries-old prayer is a *bit* over the top. It's just a prayer, after all. Surely, even if we did understand how it was taken originally, it would not change much of what is important to us on our current faith journey! My life is taken up with making a living and caring for family. I have little time left over for esoteric explorations of ancient prayers."

"Okay, that's exactly how I'll start our study." Let me take a deep breath here, because this is important. "In the first chapter I will examine more carefully how our lifestyles have left us little time for outside interests and even less imagination for alternate meanings for an ancient prayer."

"Aha!" You caught me. "Prayer is not really a cognitive exercise. That's what you said just now. The words are simply a vehicle for the emotional urges and spiritual yearnings that lie behind them. It doesn't really matter that we don't know what the prayer is about, does it?"

"Fair enough! In the second chapter I will outline three modes of praying to set my reading of the Prayer within the classic spiritual practices of Christianity."

"Continue. I'm listening."

"This is the exciting part. Once we have laid out the details of these preliminary matters, I am going to suggest that the Prayer is all about the words that are pronounced. They are building blocks for a . . ."

"Slow down . . . give that to me slowly, please." You look alert and quizzical. "I am not sure I follow you."

"Here's what I am saying." Deep breath. "Let me put my thesis in a positive light. Whether Jesus ever uttered the words of the Prayer or not, the first community that used those words prayed this prayer to build their community. It wasn't about piety at all. The words were a *creative act*. Those first disciples of the kingdom movement of Jesus actually meant what they prayed, and they literally prayed their church into life. The words perform the acts of which they speak. I admit that this is a strange way to think about prayer, but it is a key to understanding both how the church got started back then and how it might be revived right now."

"Now you've lost me. I thought a prayer was a spiritual exercise." You pause. "Am I missing something here?"

"Not at all. It's a rethinking of prayer. Before we spiritualize these ancient words and turn daily bread on the table into nourishment for the soul and financial debt into the weight of guilt, let's give these phrases full measure. Why not allow the words to stand as they were first pronounced, not with hidden spiritual meanings but with concrete political ones?"

"Go on."

"As I mentioned above, our problem is that the Prayer is too easy. We know it too well. Like a joke told over and over again, the punch line can no longer surprise us. We are recipients of two millennia of interpretation that has served to tell us what to think of the Prayer before we begin and in consequence has domesticated what was a very political and very disturbing selection of words."

You are on the edge of your seat. "How are you going to prove this?"

"In the chapters that follow the basic elaboration of my thesis, our challenge will be to avoid the temptation to think we know what we're praying. It's more than a bit of Second Temple piety. Let's not let the simplicity of the Prayer fool us into disregarding it as a lightweight within the theological arena. The Prayer is a very serious and deep undertaking. Its few, frank lines capture and inspire an entire system of being: an alternate reality and a community that lived it.

"So, through the final chapters of this text, I will take each line of the Prayer one at a time. It will be evident that through this prayer Jesus invited his disciples to live a new life in two interrelated ways. First, the Prayer lays out an economic ideology which, until recently, was seen as idealist and utopian, but has strangely become quite relevant in recent decades. Known as 'Jubilee economics,' the Prayer outlines a financial program based on the principle that the gap between rich and poor should never be allowed to grow. The Prayer is a pledge that the distance between destitution and abundance will become shorter with time. Those who are slaves to debt should be liberated and all people should have enough bread to survive each day. In this sense, the Jesus Prayer is arguing that some basic human needs need to be lifted out of the economic realm entirely. There are some things that are not for sale: human survival chief among them.

"In the second place, the Prayer was the watchword for an alternate political reality. Not just a spiritual entity or utopian dream, the early Christian circle, which the author of the Gospel of Luke called 'the way,' was a full-blown society—grounded and growing. It had a self-understanding that stood in stark contrast to the governing principles of the Empire.

"The conquering Romans required very little of their subjugated peoples apart from allegiance to the theology that informed their *Pax Romana*. To be a good citizen, one had to do due homage to the cult of the emperor, worship his divinity, and pay lip service to the idea that peace (whatever that might have meant at the time) comes through the ultimate triumph of the Roman legions.

"The Christians who prayed the Prayer refused to give that allegiance to the Empire, not just to the obvious imperial mythos like the cult of emperor worship, but the entire imperial project. They were citizens of God's empire, not Caesar's. However, their resistance did not take the form of open rebellion—fighting Rome's power with their own meager military or political resources. No, their resistance was subtler and yet more enduring. They simply refused to give the Empire their faith. They rejected the "normalcy of the civilization" (Crossan), its techniques and common sense. The Christians withheld their trust in the reigning myth of might in which social distinctions and patronage ruled. They lived out their alternative community—one that operated day by day on different principles. Their theology was that one found peace through justice.

"Of course, the attempts to embody the kingdom of God on earth were fraught with failures; nonetheless the followers of Jesus persevered for several centuries in the expansion of a kingdom of God which resisted the kingdom of Caesar.

"And when they prayed—and they apparently did it often—the followers of Jesus were doing more than sky-gazing or wish-weaving. The Prayer was fulfillment and blessing. It was an act of establishing their community. These sixty-eight words changed their world. Unlike modern prayers that appear to be the litany of petitions, a selection of choice requests that we hope God will fulfill in some distant time and place—much like Santa Claus does for young children today—they literally prayed their living into existence.

"That's my thesis in a nutshell. The petitions of the Prayer were used to shape a new reality for those who first prayed them. The original audience was praying their community into life. Not a fiction, not whistling in the dark. The Prayer was a concrete and tangible exercise, a constructive act. By common consent, the Prayer was praying God's household into existence— a real living home—a household as real as the ones that preoccupy and sustain us today."

"Right," you say, "that was a pretty long answer to a simple question. Are you done?"

"We're just beginning."

1

What is "our living"?

Fighting against Time

"Why did I not see it before?"

That's what you said when you caught a glimpse of the backyard in the morning sunlight, a vista that you had never taken time to appreciate before. It's been there forever. The plush, fresh green of the lawn didn't blossom overnight. Likewise, the sparkle of the rising sun. Both are there, every day, waiting for you to notice. Without intending it, one morning you did. You stopped long enough and saw it—how the sun's light caught the small rivulets of dew on the blades of grass and made them twinkle ever so slightly, spreading a carpet of sparkles leading across the expanse of the lawn toward the slanted rays of the sun.

Marvelous! For a moment, your breath is short and you wonder at the beauty laid out at your feet and you gasp, "Why did I not see it before?"

Overlooking the garden is a mistake, a regrettable oversight, but what if it happens with your child. Now we're talking tragedy, capital "T."

Alas, we do that too.

My small toddler has grown into a very excitable young boy, and while he sings constantly around the house, it never occurred to me that he's musical. Then, home comes the note from the music teacher asking for a conference. "Good news, not bad!" She had scribbled at the bottom of the page. I arrive at her room, only to discover that she wants my child to be in a special choir of boys. "He has a gift," she says, smiling, "a special ear for music." As if for the first time, I hear his tiny voice mimicking all the songs on the radio.

And now I see it!

It's as if I had previously been blind to his gift. He needs to listen to a song only once and it's in his head. My mind jumps back to a recent picture of him downloading a song in Spanish from the computer, a song that I had completely forgotten about. I heard it two years ago, in a friend's backyard in Cuba. But he recalls it and can sing it too! Before I can stop myself I say, "Why did I not see it before?"

I relate this oversight to a friend and marvel. Sure, I can soothe myself with a few excuses: "He's so young, you'd not think of it. Especially for a boy. Music? Never!" Or when I weigh out the day's events before lights out, I say that I don't perceive what is right before my nose because I'm too close to see it. "The teacher has the proper distance to take note of his gift."

But the fact remains that here was the light of my heart, sprouting a very beautiful gift and I didn't even notice. It was like I was blind to the beauty of a rose growing at my feet.

This has happened to you. I know it has. And more frequently of late. We're not suffering from the onset of dementia. We are not lazy. We are victims of a treadmill life that is ticking away in overdrive, moving the seconds by us at greater and greater speeds.

Last night, I opened a favorite book and there it was again: an insight that had such clarity and meaning I found myself smiling, "Why did I not see that before?" Frances Mayes, in her second book on Tuscany, *Bella Tuscany*,[1] notes that time is held differently in Italy and California. In the former you live through it. In the latter, you fight against it.

Brilliant. Why had I not seen this before? I had certainly felt it and worked around the edges of such an insight, but I had never been struck with such a simple fact. In the North American competitive world, time is not a friend. It's the great foe.

It's as if time is a foreigner, a subversive agent bent upon our demise and destruction. We buy Daytimers, strap a Blueberry to our hip, fire up our iPhones, formulate agendas for even the most casual encounters. We do all this because time is our adversary. If we don't tackle it head on and organize it, we will lose it. If we don't manage our time, we might waste it. Such a common assumption is hardly ever questioned. Time is an adversary to be tamed and mastered. We imbue time with the mind-set of a wanton child and accept without question that it's a renegade, always wanting to run away with itself or defeat us. And if we are not vigilant, it will do just that.

---

1. Mayes, *Bella Tuscany*, 4–5.

Besides being uncontrollable like a child, time is also viewed as a ruthless warrior. How strange that we face our days like a commander waiting to do battle with time—the final enemy. We arrange our energies to strike down this tempter. We know time will get us in the end, but in the meantime, we'll not allow it to have the upper hand! Don't give an inch. We'll measure each moment to squeeze from it the exact results we want, prioritize and plan to avoid losing a strategic advantage, squandering our minutes and seconds. We program our electronic agendas to alert us of upcoming appointments so that time will not overtake us. We will drown in our over-charged days if we are not prepared in advance to do battle against the passing of the hours. Time has the power to conquer us if we do not "prioritize." Everything from writing "thank you" notes to making love is slotted into our schedule.

More than a feckless child and mighty opponent, how often do we paint time as a great Faustian tempter? If we gave time free rein, well, who knows where we would end up? We'd lose productivity, but what else? If time took over and set the pace, we'd probably find ourselves lost in a daydream maze of little delights with no clear direction or purpose. This morning, as I rose from a table at the seminary in Cuba, my companions rejoiced that we had a free morning. Immediately, people began to list the tasks they could get done in our "free time." It was as if no one would allow time to be free, for such an alluring beast would lead us down a rabbit hole. We'd be lost. When we awoke from that slumber, we'd be more frustrated and anxious than ever—having wasted the few precious, "free" moments we have been given.

So, we meet and measure out our seconds parsimoniously—not wanting to grant anything or anyone more time than they deserve. Sometimes we even rob time from our most important spaces—from our close friends and family, because we don't have time to fritter away on them while other "pressing matters" stare back at us from our date books.

When I am dying, with family members close by, a circle of smiles saying good-bye to me, do I want them to say things like:

"Boy, he really kept us on track!"

"What an absolute stickler for agenda! Never let himself get distracted from his work."

"Thank goodness he spent so much time doing his job."

No. When I die, I want to think I made a difference in the lives of those I love. And difference takes time. You don't get depth of contact with those around you just because you fit them in when you are "free." There is little benefit gained in slotting "depth" in between appointments in your Daytimer. There has to be a sincere intentionality matched by a length of time to make it take. No time, no difference.

When our children complain that we never make time for them, or when we ask at the end of a day, "Where did the time go?" may we have the insight to realize that we are fighting time rather than living it! May we have the humility to admit, "Why did I never see that before?"

I'm preaching to myself here. I can tell.

But this is not a scolding sermon, nor a text on the sociological patterns of North American lifestyles, so let me make the connection with prayer.

The first community of people following Jesus prayed their living into existence. For them there was never any separation between the two. They lived their time. They did not fight it or try to control it.

Our predicament as North American Christians is that we have made a distinct separation between *making a living* and just *living*. We have compartmentalized our lives into the time slots of our digital agendas. Believing that we were on the right track, we have placed boundaries around our homes and households, keeping business and the affairs of earning a living separate from our "real living."

What a truly dismaying prospect.

The time we take at work is never seen as one and the same as time spent building a home. It is only the lucky ones who can combine building a home with earning a living. Most people have to sacrifice time at home in order to make the money that is required to actually have one. They are never seen as one in the same thing. We have a "living" and then we have work. The purpose of one is not very closely linked to the second.

Matthew Fox, in his book on modern work styles,[2] makes this distinction in a slightly different fashion. He points out that all people have a vocation: a life purpose. Perhaps we are not aware of it, or we have long tried to ignore or even deny it. But it is there—the semi-conscious inkling or the sure realization that we have been set on this earth with a mission. Fox suggests that all human beings have a vocation, which is a gift from our Maker, from the beginning. Work does not coincide with our vocation as a matter of course. Work is what we have to do to survive—to buy food, shelter, and clothing so that we will have the ability to fulfill our vocation.

2. Fox, *The Reinvention of Work*.

Again, it is the fortunate who can combine their vocation and work into a meaningful, indivisible whole.

Whether we use Fox's categories or stick with the difference between making a living and earning a living, the point is the same. Modern lives are bifocal and this split is damaging to those who wish to live fully in the moment.

Praying a Living

Modern minds have lost any sense that prayer has a tangible and materialist aspect. To us, praying is basically a spiritual, linguistic workout. We open our hearts to God, exercise our guilt reflexes, stretch out our shortcomings, plead our regrets, and ask for forgiveness. At best, prayer is a verbal expression of our intention to lead a new life. Or it has become a contemplative "brainwashing," a time to cleanse our thoughts of self-absorption in order to ready our hearts for God's indwelling. At worst, prayer devolves into a mindless bit of verbiage, a filler that you insert between hymns and sermons.

However, if we unmask how we have reduced the Lord's Prayer to personal piety, we may be able to rekindle the fires that inspired a new religious movement and changed human history. Consequently, we may revive our own personal experience of religion and find a meaningful direction in our journey through life.

Here's our challenge. Can we reappropriate the Lord's Prayer as it was understood by Jesus and his followers? Can we do more than "pray words"? Can we pray our community into life?

I think of the Lord's Prayer as a foundation. It was the building block on which the community constructed itself. You returned to this safe structure every day because it gave you your life, real bread, and hope. You came to this prayer for the reassurance that you would not starve. You turned to it when you were overwhelmed by doubts or frightened by persecutions. From the Lord's Prayer, you gained strength when you were challenged or drained. It built you into whom you would become.

Why can't we do the same?

Unlike the North American variants of Christianity, the first circles of "Jesus people" used prayer as the actual establishment of their movement. Through it, by common consent, they built God's reign here on earth. They prayed the community of God into life. They prayed their living.

I don't know how else to say it without being misunderstood. Christians prayed their household *into reality*. They did not pray *for* a living, as if it was a reality to be granted sometime in the future—a petition that would eventually be fulfilled. Their prayer was not like that. Disciples of Jesus prayed their living, they made it happen. Prayer was a community-building process, a real flesh-and-blood community relying on spiritual overtones, perhaps, but focusing on the here and now of daily life. In that sense, it was a living prayer—a prayer that brought into reality a new way of living.

In this book, I use the word *living* in at least two ways. First, the Lord's Prayer was like "praying a living" because it shaped and reshaped a new structure of human existence and human community. After you sat in a circle with the Prayer, your life was never the same. Second, it embodied a new way to garner the resources to survive from one day to the next. It represented a living wage and a new way to support yourself and your family.

Does this kind of praying make any sense? To the modern mind, the Lord's Prayer is just words. Beautiful words, but words nonetheless. That is our post-Enlightenment understanding of the power of uttered words and what they can do and can't do.

We *know* without doubt that the actual words of a prayer can't transform our lives—not on their own. But that ancient community had a different knowledge and expectation. They knew another way of using words—a way we have largely forgotten in the twenty-first century. It's this forgotten mode of spiritual and material discourse that I wish to examine in the latter chapters of this text and promote as our way forward as believers.

In the meantime, each Sunday I stand behind the communion table and begin that ancient prayer. I have a deep regret, a sense that we got it all wrong, that we misunderstood the entire project. Like my alphabet in first grade, we mouth or mutter the words, but we are getting the meaning backwards.

This book is my simple attempt to get the meanings of the words right, or at least to point toward some old meanings in ancient language that can serve as new directions for modern living.

The Growth of the Kingdom Movement

Before we examine the Prayer itself, let us place it in the "matrix"[3] of first-century Palestine. What was the lived reality of the initial audience of Jesus?

3. John Dominic Crossan uses this term in current lectures and in his text written

Whenever they heard him speak of a "kingdom of God," what did they imagine he meant? How did they go about living out his vision? Likewise, how did the Prayer enhance this incarnation of Jesus' mission?

There are three facts that dominated the sociopolitical and spiritual landscape of those who first gathered around Jesus. Keep in mind that while twenty-first–century believers might want to separate spirituality and social context, in the first century world they are one in the same—two sides of the same coin, so to speak.

First, picture occupied territory. Approximately half a century before the birth of Christ, the Romans marched over the hill behind Nazareth. By the time Jesus began his Galilean preaching mission, it looked like they were a permanent fixture. Within recent memory, a relatively small and ill-fated rebellion had taken place. It happened somewhere around the date of Christ's birth. So, most of his audience would have had firsthand experience of what an occupying force can do.

When the legions came down from Damascus to quell revolt, they left nothing living in their wake. Their commanders were angry, for in order to deal with some peasant malcontents, they left the eastern flank of the Empire vulnerable to attack. They were therefore determined to deliver a lesson that would not be easily forgotten. The devastation was complete. So, let us never forget that lively memories of that mini-apocalypse colored the collective consciousness of the audience of Jesus.

When the Romans came to stay, it changed everything. Now any action was construed as a political one. All that happened held dual significance. If you went about your business, then you were either acquiescing to Roman oppression or resisting the Empire by making a living despite their oppressive taxes. Nothing was without meaning. Every act was interpreted in relation to the occupation forces. Again, if you fulfilled your temple rituals, you were at the same time collaborating with the traitorous priestly aristocracy and upholding the monotheistic beauty of Judaism in the face of Roman civil religion. All actions were open to interpretation and even the smallest gesture was potentially explosive.

So, we should imagine a fearful, discontented populace. Resentment simmered just below the surface. Few could openly voice opposition to Roman rule and even fewer had the courage or opportunity to act on it.

---

with Marcus Borg, *The First Paul.* Avoiding the term *context,* Crossan wishes to describe the many-layered interrelationship between an imperial world and the evolving Christian reality. They are no static entities, but constantly interacting ones.

I take it for granted that, when it comes to imperial authority exercised either directly through military force or administered by the collaborating local aristocracy, all peasants were resisters. Of course, they had little chance of armed resistance and therefore their opposition to the occupying forces would be understated: finding most vibrant expression in campfire jokes, subtle, coded symbolic gestures of defiance and reluctant, minimalist compliance.

The second fact: it is essential to see the time of Jesus as an inter-bellum time. Almost equally distant from two armed uprisings, the ministry of Jesus flourished during a time of relative tranquility.

No . . . that is misleading. It would be better to note that the itinerancy of Jesus was possible, for there was no serious armed resistance to the Romans while he walked the shore of the inland sea. It was either impossible or not contemplated. The most recent example of any organized resistance was the prophetic, nonviolent civil disobedience of John the Baptizer. But his ministry was directed more pointedly at Herod Antipas, a Roman puppet, and so was more like an arm's length resistance to Rome.

It was not the threat of physical violence that dominated the domestic/spiritual landscape. People feared for their lives of course—as we all do—but the day-to-day pressure came from another source: taxes. They were the chief burden, the tangible testimony to Roman authority. Rising taxes were the storm clouds on the horizon. Just as fear of nuclear war shaped a generation in the twentieth century, and global warming molds that of the twenty-first century, the dual weight of loans and taxation threatened to bury the vast majority of peasants in first-century Palestine in a mudslide of dismay and despair.

The Roman Empire expanded following a predictable pattern: militarization for the purpose of expanding Roman commercial interests and culture. With no armed resistance to interrupt this pattern, the years preceding the itinerant preaching missions of Jesus witnessed greater commercialization of land and higher levels of consistent taxation—both of agriculture and aquaculture.

Antipas, the Tetrarch of southern Galilee, was trying to replicate the splendor of his father, Herod the Great. Just as Herod had built Caesari Maratima in honor of Augustus, Antipas moved his capital from Sephoris (four kilometers from Nazareth) to the inland seashore. There he built a new capital city, Tiberias, a tribute to the current emperor, Tiberius. To pay for this plan, taxes were levied and increased. More than likely, the fishing trade—which had enjoyed exemption from Roman interference—was then subjected to licenses, penalties, and restrictions.

Can you imagine the social dislocation that taxes imposed? In that world, fishing was the peasants' last resort, a final chance to stave off starvation. With Antipas, that window of opportunity was closed. Who cared about where the taxes went or what they bought? To peasants, the architectural feats of splendor, whether in Tiberias or Jerusalem, were just another humiliating reminder of their impotence and vulnerability. Taxes trailed scarcity in their wake and imposed tangible hunger at home.

Likewise, old patterns of land tenure were collapsing under the double weight of taxation and debt. Where once the vast majority of peasants lived on small acreages, subsisting on their own land, there is sufficient archeological evidence to support the premise that the commercialization of the Roman empire caused a serious disruption in that ancient pattern.[4] The greed of rulers and the need to produce greater levels of surplus for the building projects of the mighty was bearing down on the lower class, who made up the vast majority of the population.

As taxation systems began to put pressure on traditional farming practices to produce larger surpluses, peasant farmers found themselves laboring for an overlord or vineyard owner—trying to create value that could be used to pay off their tax burdens.

As it became impossible to sustain adequate crop yields, peasants resorted to loans, using their farms as collateral. As the economic pressure built, land was forfeited. For peasants, the land was God's bounty, a sacred trust. They held their land as divine gift. It was a source of spiritual pride and legal standing. Without land, they were bankrupt, humiliated, and disenfranchised. As farmers lost their land because of crop failure or through bad debts, they were thrust into the full-blown separation between home and work. Their time was no longer their own. They had to sell their time, working each hour to get the resources they needed to support the home.

Can you now picture the circle of faces who gather around Jesus? Everyone is angry with Roman rules, feeling betrayed by local clan overlords and uncertain of the God of their salvation. Ancient and sacred structures of land tenure are in doubt. Likewise, God's justice seems questionable. This resentment and dismay is colored by a third fact to keep in mind: shame.

---

4. Here I draw heavily on Crossan's work written with Jonathan Reed: *Excavating Jesus*.

First-century Palestine was built on a system of valuation in honor as the chief means of exchange while shame was the primary penalty. This will require some pages to explain. Perhaps you'd like to get a coffee and relax a bit with this idea.

Imagine the modern Western society and ask, "How do we designate what is worthy?" The simple answer is: "money." Anything of value has a price tag. We designate our sense of importance by linking it to a monetary figure. Of course, we treasure love and compassion, but our world speaks money—every avenue of human activity to colored by it. Justice? We inspire right behavior through a system of monetary rewards and penalties. Love? Families spend their days accumulating a bank account and its size reflects relative importance. Trust? We give out honorary degrees to great philanthropists who donate large sums of money to their pet projects. On and on it goes. Our world pays singular homage at the temple of money, places it as the supreme arbiter of worth.

Now, let us not get defensive. I am not making a judgment on money as a vehicle for valuation. It's just the reality of our current world. It cannot be ignored, and indeed anyone who would analyze our modern world would be foolish if they ignored this foundational principle.

If we move back into the matrix of the first century, we are traveling down a different path of valuation. In that world, "honor" is the chief purveyor of worth. A family was not counted "good" because of their money or land—though these things were important. It was the accumulated *honor* they possessed that mattered. Often personified in the person of the clan patriarch, honor was gold.

Unlike coins and bills, honor was not a simple medium of exchange. It was an amalgam of historical respect, spiritual authority, current family dynamics, private deals, and public prejudices. One's honor was not material, but it was tangible. You could not add up honor with a calculator, but it was bankable.

Honor was conferred in the public sphere. Peasants gave it to their overlords through open obedience. Equals shared and exchanged honor through an unspoken system of mutual respect and favors. Sons obeyed fathers in the field and daughters listened to mothers in the kitchen. Patriarchs offered extravagant hospitality to underlings who were equally extravagant in their compliments of their *Kyrie*, their Lord. Of course, a family's honor was linked to its righteousness. So, a family that observed the yearly sacrificial rites in Jerusalem was revered. Likewise, a purification pool, stone cooking implements, and prayer practices would reinforce clan honor.

Often it was the patriarch who embodied the honor of his family. His dignity and wisdom were revered. As long as he tended and stewarded his ancestral lands, provided food and security to his kinfolk, his honor was never in doubt.

Shame was the underside of the honor system. If, horror of horrors, children disobeyed parents or peasants withheld their devotion (or taxes), a family's honor was tainted and shamed. Any loss of face or material standing held the sting of humiliation. Lose your family's land and your honor would take a near-fatal blow.

Just as honor was conferred in the town square, shame also operated in the open marketplace. Unlike the modern world, where a person's net worth is held as a personal secret, one's worth in first-century Palestine was everyone's business. This creates a problem. If one loses honor though a shameful act—a son disobeying the father, for instance—then this honor can only be reinstated through a public act of vengeance. No private deals.

The honor/shame system of valuation fits hand in glove with the basic approach to agency in that culture. To get something done one used a patronage system. Unlike a democratic society, in the matrix of Jesus' society there was no assumption of immediate access. If you were in need, you went to your overlord and asked for a favor. That was how you showed honor to the head of your family. This patron then went to his overlord, and so the request was sent up a ladder of favors and counter-favors until an answer was achieved and sent back down the food chain. One's honor determined a place in this system.

Patronage based on honor commanded the audience of Jesus. They assumed without rancor that this was how God intended the world to operate. Whether in the temple, palace, household, or workshop, it was the same pattern. Given the essential character of one's honor, there was no questioning of the need for revenge: once honor is lost, it can only be claimed back through exacting vengeance on the one who has taken it away. Forgiveness is impossible. There is no upside to forgiving an opponent. Not only will it be perceived as weakness, it will not achieve the desired end of restoring equilibrium to the social system. The cycle of attack and revenge is therefore an entirely moral, unquestionable necessity.

To enter into the days of the Lord's Prayer is to accept these three facts: Roman occupation, murderous taxation, and mounting shame.

But these are just words. Stand as Jesus did, before a collection of first-century peasants and fishers, and the influences of these facts are writ large. You can see it in their eyes, pain mingled with anger and humiliation. The Romanization of Galilee meant a disruption in old traditions: one of the reasons for the growing unrest among the under classes and their interest in the kingdom movement of Jesus. When the carpenter from Nazareth showed up on the shores of the Sea of Galilee, we can imagine him talking with fishers who had lost the ability to fish—having no boat or no means to pay the tariffs to go out onto the lake.[5] Likewise, the peasant farmers from the north who had lost their land would have stood shoulder to shoulder with a growing resentment that the Romans had robbed their land and undermined their ability to make a decent living and feed their families. They had therefore mocked the God of Israel, who seemed impotent or indifferent. Once there was land, and each family made its way on its own piece of earth. Now they had to earn it, and that meant walking the knife edge of scarcity. One misstep and they and their families were lost.

To touch their dismay and frustration, we have to see that the people who flocked to Jesus were suffering from two humiliations. When the family farm was lost or seriously compromised, people felt their land had been taken from them or corrupted. Their means of life, the basic principle of making a living, were put into jeopardy. Life grew more precarious when tenuous work arrangements were the sole means for survival. To add insult to injury, their dignity and self-worth were tinged by the shame of betraying God's command to tend the land, to treat it as a holy trust.

The people who surround Jesus are angry, feeling pressured, cut off from their means of self-worth, and desperate to earn a living. A revolution in the making! When I look around the crowd that we know were present as Jesus preached, I am never surprised that the first century witnessed several small acts of open resistance to Rome and at least one very serious revolt. It was not difficult to stir a crowd into dissent. What is most striking is how well and consistently Jesus resisted the temptation to use their unrest to further his cause. In those circumstances, his pacifist approach to resistance, as it attested in Matthew's Sermon on the Mount (Matt 5:38), is quite remarkable.

That Jesus chose not to advocate open resistance to Rome must be seen as more than a secondary subplot or tangential idea. It's too easy to start a

---

5. For a greater exploration of this phenomenon, see Crossan and Reed, *Excavating Jesus*, 85–87, 113–15.

war. Violence is not hard. It is often the first response when conditions grow too onerous to bear. Jesus' unwillingness to give in to the obvious desires of crowds to get some relief from their suffering by venting their animosity with swords and bloodletting—it is extraordinary.

The pacifism of Jesus is therefore more than a social coincidence or personal aberration. It is the foundation of his movement: a conscious, consistent, nonviolent resistance to empire. When we come close to the nonviolent, resistant character of the "kingdom movement" of Jesus, we can hear the heartbeat of his strategic genius and spiritual strength.

It is unfortunate that theologians and church leaders have not recognized this fact. We take the pacifism of Jesus as an obvious corollary to the individualized mission we have imputed to his preaching. If he wasn't advocating war—and he wasn't—then we assumed he intended a "kingdom" of another kind when he spoke of its coming. In that sense, we depoliticized his movement and domesticated his parables and preaching. I believe we have mistakenly believed that Jesus' kingdom was literally "not of this world" (John 18:36). It happens above and beyond history. One suffered the Caesars of this earthly realm, because the real point was to reach the reign of Christ waiting in the next life.

Our danger is that we intrude on first-century culture with post-Enlightenment thinking. We accept the separation of the material and spiritual when no such distinction existed for Jesus. We see miraculous or spiritual existence to be distinct from daily life. For modern people, heaven exists above and beyond history. For Jesus, God was a very "here-and-now" reality. Prayer was not distinct from making a living. They were the same, and one's daily routine would never be seen separate from one's devotion to God.

As a further distortion of the initial intentions of Jesus, North Americans have naturally reduced his words to an individual level. We have linked the idea of "salvation" inextricably to the notion of the "personal life." Our logic is colored by a second unquestioned dualism: the distinction of personal and political. There is a spiritual personal dimension to life and then the collective political realm—discrete facts of human life. When we read that Jesus would not, or could not, take on the Romans and did not advocate violence, we automatically presume that his purpose must have been to preach a spiritual, individual, and personal redemption.

This sort of reasoning gave rise to the theory of the two realms—one on earth ordained by God which we do not resist, and one in heaven over which Christ rules.

However, what if Jesus meant to promote resistance? If he was moved by the people's plight and thought that the rule of Caesar was injurious and unjust, surely, he would want to offer some form of resistance? Let us imagine that Jesus was as human as the next man. He witnessed and learned from the mistakes of others. He watched what happened to John's baptizing mission and how easily it was for a tyrant literally to cut it down. So, what could be done? How would you speak of resistance while the occupying forces are breathing down the neck of your next sermon? If you cannot block out the cries of the people, what would you suggest? A tense, pressing dilemma, one that any self-respecting prophet could not hope to avoid. You want to earn your spurs in first-century Palestine, you have to face the Roman question.

As we open the Gospels, I would have us feel this tension. It is not the record of pretty religious sentiments—the parlor games of preachers who have too much time on their hands. This is the tale of nail-biting times, when you couldn't avoid the impossible dream of freedom from hunger and destitution.

Come back one last time to the place from which Jesus is preaching. As you look across the crowd, you can taste their hardship. You see a mother's downward gaze as she mourns the growing starvation of her babies. You look into the eyes of weathered fishers and see years of corroding humiliation. In the eyes of young people, you can see the flickering fires of rebellion. And you ask yourself, "What can I say that will make any difference? How can I lead these people to a real and sustainable solution—without getting us all killed in a futile attempt to openly resist the Roman legions?"

The Lord's Prayer as Resistance

Would you invite people to pray?

That's what Jesus did. Not as avoidance. It was not a head-in-the-sand response. The Prayer was a blueprint for resistance. It became not only a plan, but an invocation of an alternate way to resist Rome.

Why not recite the Lord's Prayer now, and as you do, imagine that it is a formula for resistance to the powers over our lives that want to separate us from our living. It is the invocation of a time when we don't fight time, but live through it. A prayer that reunites our work and vocation.

"Can one prayer really do all that?" you ask.

"Yes," I reply. "And so much more."

The Prayer will reorder our living: how we structure our community "living," setting a new standard for how we garner the resources to survive from one day to the next. It spells out to the path to a living wage and therefore revitalizes those who speak it.

All that and so much more!

2

What is "our praying"?

"Teach Us to Pray"

I SAID THAT I was a professional "pray-er." That's what ministers do. We pray. So, you might find it curious that recently I refused to do it. Pray? I just couldn't do it.

Sitting in a crowd of over 600 people, I was involved in a new form of contemplative worship, feeling my way into some peculiar words and practices, when the officiant told us of his experience in Guatemala where whole congregations would pray out loud. No surprise there, Christians often do that. What's the Lord's Prayer except that?

But the officiant added that everyone in that Latin American audience was praying his or her own prayer. There's no uniformity of ideas of phraseology, just hundreds of distinct and individual prayers, all spoken at once in a chaotic soup of words. At first it sounded like spiritual anarchy, and then it became the like an ocean of petitions—the varied and beautiful waves of ideas flowing toward the creator—all at the same time.

"So," says the presider at the front, "Let's do that now." He stepped back from the microphone and began his own prayer and the rest of us remained silent. This was an idea outside our ken. Why would we all spontaneously begin our own prayers out loud? Surely this would be confusing to God. We sat silent.

After an awkward pause, the patient officiant reminded us of what we were to do. "Just utter your own prayer. Don't worry what someone else is saying. It's all about you speaking your own truth to God." He looked meaningfully at us and added, "Just do it now!" He stepped back a second time, and we did what he asked. Well, most of us did. Six hundred different prayers began. Tentatively at first and then more boldly. A host of names were uttered with reverence and reference to their needs. There were scattering references to world events or current issues for our circle.

Yet, I couldn't find the courage to join in. How could I speak my personal prayers into the crowd of other spoken prayers? It seemed impolite! Like I was interrupting my neighbor in his serious conversations with God. But sitting silent was also embarrassing. I was listening to another's petitions and not knowing if I should. Was I hearing something too intimate, too personal?

It was then that I realized prayer is a peculiar human activity. Like singing, it comes naturally enough to every race and clan. But it is curious nonetheless. Imagine us! We speak words out loud, or think them silently, and we believe we are communicating with the Creator of the Universe! Forget calling the White House or texting the Queen—we're getting in touch with the One who made heaven and earth! (Psalm 121:2).

Me? Talk to God?

How utterly incredible and yet how universally satisfying!

It's only when we pause during the praying reflex and appreciate the absolute bold-faced lunacy of what we are doing that the act of praying becomes a mystery we want to understand. If we slow ourselves down and don't follow the crowd to fold our hands and bow our heads, the question of "how" becomes more serious. "How do we pray?"

The first followers of Jesus had just such an opportunity and voiced that question. "Lord," they said, "teach us how to pray!" (Luke 11:1).

Now, I find it difficult to imagine that they didn't know the basics of praying. It's not a stretch to imagine that some of that audience had been to the sacred sites in Jerusalem and heard the priests in the temple. When they had been to the synagogue gathering, they would have witnessed their share of praying. And for the devout who celebrated Passover, they surely would have uttered the prescribed prayers. Clearly, though, they were not satisfied. The prayers they had seen or heard left them unfulfilled. Even if they felt their prayers had been meaningful, they believed that Jesus, who spoke with authority, would have a better take on that common practice. Surely this spiritual man would shed some light on what had hitherto been a mysterious or less than meaningful enterprise.

"Teach us how to pray."

In response to that question in Luke, Jesus immediately recites the Prayer. No commentary. You want to pray? Here, say this prayer and you will do it properly.

Matthew's recounting of the same event occurs within the Sermon on the Mount (Matt 6: 5–13): Jesus begins with a few qualifications about praying, all of which culminate in the reciting of the famous lines of the Prayer.

Before we get to that actual Prayer, let's look at Jesus' suggestions. He essentially makes two points: Prayer is not a show and it is not fluff.

No Show!

> And when you pray, don't act like phonies. They love to pray in houses of worship and on street corners, so they can show off in public . . . . When you pray, go into a room by yourself and shut the door behind you. Then pray to your Father, the hidden one. And your Father with an eye for the hidden will applaud you. (Matt 6:5–6)

The followers of Jesus would have seen the professional, public "pray-ers," the real deal in action. I think we can imagine that many were sincere and faithful in lifting the pain of the earth up to heaven. However, there must have been enough "phonies" among the genuine that people had a common caricature of the false "pray-ers." They stand out, quite literally, because it is on the street corner that they want to put on a show of spirituality. They don't hide their light under a bushel. Jesus suggested that these phonies love the limelight. They want to be seen as pious and they used prayer as an ego boost. Praying out in the open was a way to attract attention to themselves and the content of their prayers. It was a show of piety intended to gain status and respectability for one who did the praying. Prayer had devolved into a performance!

After complaining about the phonies and their pious show, Jesus suggests that you should go into a closet, because your God, who is as close you as a father, is also "the hidden one." Don't rush past that assertion. What a dramatic statement: God is hidden. What could Jesus possibly mean by such a statement?

I imagine there are two aspects to God's hiddenness. First, God is not easy or obvious. You don't just find God by walking up to the front door of heaven and giving the pearly gates a firm shake. While God's love is simple and all-pervasive, God is not like a book you open anywhere you like. It takes time and patience to enter into this most important and intimate of relationships. That leads to a second point: the relationship with God is difficult because he is hidden, often behind the opposite of what we expect. The Gospel writers made the extraordinary claim (which we now take for granted) that the God of life is best seen in an instrument of torture and death, i.e., the cross.

In a similar manner, those who have walked through the valley of the shadow of death will confess that it is only in those dark, lonely places that God becomes most real. Surely this is counterintuitive. How does the author of life become more evident in the presence of death?

It is in response to that question that the Christian Scriptures, especially Mark, promote the idea of a hidden God. This becomes a key to unlocking the mysterious miracles of the first Christian gatherings.

But we get ahead of ourselves.

For now, let us accept that prayer is a "hidden" affair. Call it a humble conversation. A modest or self-effacing venture, prayer points away from itself to the One toward whom it is addressed.

When I was a newly-minted pastor, I was sent to an isolated region of the province of Québec, right on the Atlantic coast. Once settled, I made friends with the local Pentecostal minister. We had many families that attended both of our churches, so it made sense to cooperate in our ministry.

One week, we cosponsored a series of seminars about speaking in tongues. An "expert" from the big city came out to teach us what it was supposed to be like and how it was intended to function. Excellent training and very helpful to someone like myself, who had cut his teeth on liberal interpretations of Christianity and the decorum of public worship. This was wild . . . when we prayed it was more like "ranting" than "praying."

After the final night, we met at my friend's house for tea and cake, to celebrate the success of our mission. Picture us in a humble dining room, seated around the set table: the Pentecostal pastor and his wife, the outside mission leader and his wife, me by myself, warming cake and the steeping tea. I was about to dig into the goodies when the outsider suggested we should "give thanks to God" for all our blessings.

Chastised and a bit ashamed, I joined hands with the others for a blessing of our snack. The evangelist began with words I could understand and very quickly switched into speaking tongues. The Pentecostal pastor, not to be left behind, began also to pray in tongues. Then the two women. Four voices all raised to God, uttering words that made no cognitive sense, minute by minute rising higher and higher in pitch and deeper and deeper in fervor. I was the only who was silent, sitting in a swirl of sounds.

It lasted for fifteen minutes. At times, I thought I was caught in the midst of expletives that had a quasi-sexual quality. Other times it felt like a hymn sing run amok. I just wanted to get to the food. By the time the fires in the other four went out, the tea was cold and the cake was drying up.

Speaking in tongues has a legitimate and ancient place with the practice of Christian worship. No argument. It is a great gift for those who possess it. But Paul warns us not to let this gift get in the way of others. That's what was happening to me at that meal-time blessing. This was not prayer, it was a show. The longer it went on, the more I thought we were no longer speaking to God but were trying hard to impress each other with our religious zeal.

It wasn't just the public nature of some prayers that made them false. Jesus goes on to make commentary on the length of pagan prayers.

No Fluff!

> And when you pray, you should not babble on as the pagans do. They imagine that the length of their prayers will command attention. So, don't imitate them. After all, your Father knows what you need before you ask. (Matt 6:7–8)

I find it quite remarkable that the prayers with too many words are associated in the mind of Jesus with the pagans. Or perhaps this is Matthew, the third-generation Christian, putting ideas onto the lips of Jesus. Perhaps the people of Matthew's circle were familiar with the competition down the street, the local temple where public prayers were a civic necessity and hence had a rather longish quality. Maybe the pagans were known for excessive prayers because, unlike those of the Judean faith, they had many deities to address.

Whatever the reason, Jesus warns against too many words. They are not necessary. After all, God already knows what you need! Do you think that adding a few more adjectives and adverbial phrases will catch the Almighty's attention more than a few choice, brief petitions?

The "KISS principle," that works for the army, works for prayer: Keep It Simple, Stupid. During the "dirty thirties," there was a rather zealous priest who charged straight out from his seminary training onto the bald prairies. He was bent on making his mark and whipping the rural church into shape—instilling in them the fire from heaven and the rekindling of the true church. This disciple of Christ had many books that he loved, but none was more essential than his prayer book. He had his suit jacket fitted with a pocket that fit this precious text perfectly, and our man of the cloth needed little if any invitation to open it and utter whatever prayers seemed to be needed at the time.

Such is the long-suffering patience of the small country church that they can welcome and be hospitable to any variety of Christian pastor—no matter how perverted their ways. Such was the strength of this pastor's parish that they came to love their new leader despite his long-suffering prayers.

To give him his due, this new seminarian was sincere in his desire to love the people in turn. He could see their suffering as their farms were literally blown away. The lifeblood of the community was being swept away as the erosion of top soil left the land denuded of grasses for animals and trees for shade. Farmers were despairing. Banks were foreclosing. Families were disintegrating.

On one afternoon's visit to a local farm, the pastor's heart was particularly touched. A sheep farmer was losing his herd. They were dying of thirst. The farmer had little enough even for his family to drink. But he brought out a little cup of tea to slake the pastor's thirst. In gratitude and to fill the silence that ensued, the young man suggested that they might pray to God for assistance. "Perhaps a prayer for rain, or water, would be in order." And he reached into his jacket for his prayer book.

The farmer stopped him mid-gesture and said, "Before you pray, Father, why don't you come with me to see my herd." They went out into the unrelenting heat and passed the dry well, out to the paddock behind the barn. It was hidden from the farmhouse, but here in the corral were hundreds of bleating, dying sheep. No question, this was a bloodless slaughter—death by inches as the sheep panted, bleated, choked, and finally fell silent as their voices were strangled for lack of fluid.

Horrible. Words could not describe their suffering.

The priest looked at the farmer and saw, in the tightened muscles in the set of his jaw and the hardness of his gaze, that he too was dying slowly with his animals. He was supposed to be their guardian and a shepherd. Wasn't that a biblical mandate? Yet he could do nothing.

Finally, the farmer turned, looking at the priest, he said, "Father, if you can pray better than these sheep, go right ahead."

Words are never enough! You need them. But prayer is not a quantitative endeavour. Look to your heart. Our task as "pray-ers" is to be attentive to our deepest emotions, for we feel in our hearts what our reason cannot yet understand. And then we express it as simply as we can. Leave the prayer towers and the 24/7 prayer lines to the pagans. They have their reward. Your God knows what you need. Just say it and be attentive. Listen to the spirit moving in you. Speaking can be brief, but the listening to God's word in our hearts—*that* we must never cut short.

So, we have the two warnings from Jesus. Don't make prayer a show of piety and don't add fluff to the simple facts and feelings. Having these two cautions of what prayer *is not* about, can we now progress to what it *is*? Are there positive categories or varieties of prayer?

There are three basic types: contemplative, cognitive, and intercessory prayers.

Prayer as a Spiritual Workout

I'm listening to music right now.

Of course, you have no idea of this. You're just reading my words. But as I write, I have music playing . . . constantly. Right now, it's Enya singing, "Who can say where your love grows?" Haunting! The next song? I think it's Elvis who will croon that "Wise men say only fools rush in." Great!

When IBM produced a laptop computer with a built-in CD drive, my life was complete. What more could I ask for? To write with earphones in place is pure joy. The music blocks out the washing machine, the street traffic, and even my cellphone's ringtone—that's perfect! Of course, the parent in me asks how I can concentrate with all the booming distractions of loud love songs blaring in my ears. Surely, I will get confused or distracted. The fact that I don't change the music very often—sometimes I'll listen to the same CD for weeks at a time while I write—is a further problem. How can I stand it, the boring predictable melodies raining down on my senses for hours at a time?

Truth be told, I need the music.

In the first place, it's like a drug, inducing a trance-like concentration on the task at hand. Without the presence of the songs, I wouldn't be able to write so quickly or carefully. I recall one day when I arrived at my favorite coffee shop, where I love to write, and found that I had forgotten to bring along the necessary CD. I didn't want to go all the way back home to fetch it, wasting valuable writing time. So, I sat in unusual silence and began my work. It was painful! I felt like every paragraph was closer to putting my finger in a manual meat grinder and cranking the handle slowly. That's how difficult it was to get the words to come out on the screen.

Without the music, I couldn't focus. Not only could I then hear too many distractions, I was also more restless, wanting more breaks and having to stretch more often. The music serves to quell my otherwise restless energy and keep me at my writing without distraction.

Then there is the beauty of the melody and tone of the music. There's more to my music than its ability to soothe my squirming soul. It's also an aid to inspiration—but not in a *quid pro quo* fashion. There's no direct connection that I can identify. It's much more ethereal, the music's power is more elusive. I can't name exactly when and how it works—it just does.

You see, it's not that the music conveys a specific message. Of course, from time to time it gives me indirect inspiration—I'll take a line from a favorite song and weave it into the sentences at hand. But more often than not, the melodies that help me so much are more like grease in the machinery of my creativity than content.

Even while admitting that I cannot explain how the tunes contribute to my writing, its importance cannot be denied. In a way that I cannot pinpoint, the music adds a quality of depth, a coloring that is pleasing and necessary to the final outcome.

Peace for the uneasy heart and a nonverbal inspiration—have I not just described the most ancient form of prayer? Prayer began as a meditative, trance-like undertaking in which we commune with the mystery beyond our understanding. Even still today, Christians use prayer to clear the mind and as the doorway into nonverbal exploration of life's meaning and direction.

When I begin the Prayer, church people automatically join in. It doesn't really matter when or where. We could be in a hospital room, funeral parlor, or the sanctuary. The words are ingrained in our hearts, and because we can recite them without thinking, the Prayer becomes a vehicle for suspending reason. The phrases, like my background music, pave the

way to a realm where cognitive reasoning is superseded by spiritual en-
lightenment. In a way that makes no logical sense, but is true nonetheless,
when our mouths are busy mouthing the words to which we do not have
to pay attention, our minds are freed to float. I imagine that the reciting of
familiar phrases wipes our hearts clean so that we rise into another level of
consciousness. It is through the sacred space that the Prayer creates in us
that we can integrate ourselves into the universal and inscrutable mystery
we call God.

In its first and fundamental usage, prayer is all about attaining this
surreal realm. Of course, it can be a means for cognitive reasoning, but
prayer as meditation has a much richer heritage.

Prayer that is communion in the mystery beyond words and thoughts
is more than communication. It happens at another level and for a different purpose. This kind of prayer is both floating above our lives and also
drifting deeper within our souls. And its purpose is to commune with the
depth of time.

To be accurate, let's call this kind of prayer "trans-rational communion."

It's at this point that words fail me. How can I describe a reality beyond the power of reason to describe? Metaphors are our best hope. Prayer
is like the reset button in computer programs. It reconfigures all of the
settings back to their original places so that the electronics can function
as they were intended. Or perhaps prayer is a nonchemical, mind-altering
substance that relaxes our pedestrian anxieties in such a way as to enable
us to see what had otherwise been invisible. Try this: prayer is spiritual
Prozac. Too banal? How about: prayer is a soul fired workout. Your heart's
calisthenics. Too pedestrian? Well, you get the point.

In this respect, Christian prayer can take its place along other meditation techniques and practices of other faith traditions. Yoga, transcendental
meditation, Zen Buddhism—they all employ similar techniques to induce a
trans-rational state in the individual.

I can hardly downplay the importance of this kind of prayer. It is
where every prayer finally concludes. When we run out of words and the
conversation with our God stumbles and stops, when all of our anger, frustration, and fear are spent, then we enter into the mystery of God that is not
dependent on cognition. We simply live in the Almighty.

Now, let's go back to the warnings Jesus leveled at prayer in general
and ask if there is any particular caution we could raise with regard to this
kind of prayer. I can think of two issues. First, prayer is never intended to

be an escape. Jesus points out that for the "phonies" prayer is not unity with God—it's precisely an avoidance of such an encounter. They use their praying to hide in their show. Their words and actions point only to themselves.

This is not prayer. Any authentic relations with God will never allow us to stay up in the clouds. This is certainly the temptation of "trans-rational communion." In that place we are freed from daily routines, the small and great anxieties that plague us. It is so peace-filled and light-filled. Why would anyone come down? Such is the power of this kind of prayer that it is prone to escapism.

"No," says Jesus. Prayer is not about finding, achieving, and staying in a heaven above earth. Healthy spirituality brings us back to the world which God loves. That's the litmus test of any prayer practice. Ask yourself, "Does it help me to engage in the imperative ethical task of rebuilding our human community?" If it does, well done! If it doesn't? Then run—run far away from this prayer as quickly as you can, for it is false and misleading.

The second cautionary note is similar. When we start the Prayer, we begin with a community. Jesus invites us to say, "Our Father." It's not "my" Father, as if I am addressing a God who is mine alone. This prayer assumes community. We do it as a bridge to shaping a circle of prayers. Once prayer becomes only my personal exercise, I am again in danger of getting lost in my private reverie. As joyful as it may be, that is not Christian. Our prayer is not an end in itself. It does the individual no benefit if it does not lead one to embrace the neighbor *and* the enemy, and to make them part of our family.

In spite of these warnings, prayer with trans-rational communion has been underused of late within the historic churches of North America, and some effort to restore this form of prayer to our repertoire of weekly worship services and family prayer habits is being undertaken. Directed retreats, the Labyrinth, new meditative forms of prayer, longer silences in church services all help.

What more can I say? "Try it, you'll like it."

You may believe that this kind of communion is beyond you, that you can't get it. Think back to the last time you were asked to join in the Prayer after a longer prayer of intercession. Did you ask yourself what purpose the Prayer serves when it is tacked onto more elaborate and explicit vocabulary? Surely, it is redundant.

Is this not where the Prayer's nonverbal importance is made clear? The leader invites us to join with him or her "in the prayer Jesus taught us," because at that stage we move our worship beyond words. The Prayer shifts the gears of our communion with God. We leave behind our explicit concerns and rise above them to another form of communication: trans-rational communion!

But the non-rational world makes me uncomfortable. I want to know what is happening and what is required of me. So, let's move to a second form of prayer: conversations with our Maker.

Conversations with Our Maker

"Do you love me?"

How many times will I ask that in my lifetime?

I have been married for years and yet I still ask: "Do you love me?" My partner sighs and then tells me that of course she does. It usually happens when I've blown it. When I mess up at work or home, when I feel like I've let someone down, I blurt out, "Do you still love me?" Does my need to hear her affirmation mark me as a candidate for serious therapy? Maybe! Am I just an insecure, emotional wimp? Perhaps.

Have you been there, wanting to hear the three most important human words? And when your beloved resists, saying, "How often do you have to hear it? Haven't I told you before?" do you feel more despondent? Despite the fact that we have been told hundreds of times that we are worthy of love, and regardless of the fact that our beloved status has been made clear by rituals and made lasting through legal arrangements, we want to hear it again and again. There is something about hearing the words, "Yes, I love you," which is reassuring—sometimes more reassuring than a simple touch or a gift. The words of affirmation convey a reality to the sentiment that is essential.

"Do you love me?"

It is not so strange a question. As human creatures, we are anxious by our very nature. It is factory installed. We know that we live on borrowed time and that there are no certainties in life. Death stalks us all and will get us in the end. For the present, we can feel its breath on our neck and that makes us a bit skittish. So, we need regular reinforcement.

It's not just the reality of death and suffering that makes us insecure. We are also beset by feelings of guilt and recrimination. We realize that we have not and never will attain the potential we know is within us. It is to our peril that we are painfully aware of our failures. Not rocket science. Human beings are "limited." Whether we feel culpable or not, we are certainly insecure because of these limitations.

So, we ask for love. We seek constant reassurance that we are worthy of affection, that we are not alone nor will we be left to our own recourse. It is our normal and deep-seated need for reassurance that gives rise to prayer as a conversation with our Maker. We want to know, not just theoretically, but in a deeper more certain way, that we are loved and valued.

This is what I would call the need for cognitive affirmation. We pray to know that we are not alone. Our conversations with God serve that purpose. At this stage, we are not talking with our Maker to "get" anything. It is closer to a strategic retreat into the realm of God. Douglas Hall calls this type of prayer, "Thinking our way into God's presence."[1]

Of course, this "thinking our way into God's presence" can take many forms—long exhaustive prayers of thanksgiving and intercession or brief daily collects. But the Prayer holds a special place in this history of conversations with our Maker.

When we take up the Prayer, we are entering into an ancient and ongoing conversation between a Creator and the creature. It's a well-worn path, made smooth and straight by the trampling of many devout pilgrims who have gone before us. Unlike other prayers that we invent, this one has the merit of being associated with the early Jesus circle. Perhaps he crafted it himself. No matter who first coined the phrases, the fact is that the power of its simplicity keeps the conversation with our God on the right track. The Prayer keeps us focused on God and the age-old and yet very current work of bringing heaven's rule to earth.

When it is healthy, this form of prayer is like a conversation. We're joining in the give and take of communication. Quite obviously, there is only one voice being heard: ours. But it is conversation, nonetheless, since we do not presume to do all the talking. Our prayer invites the Maker to speak, to inspire us and give us guidance.

Such praying requires the skill not to say too much. It asks the "prayer" to have the discerning spirit to listen for the response of God to our words, and it asks of us that we muster the courage to allow those words of God to be critical, even judging, as well as reassuring and loving.

That is the chief point of prayer as conversation with God. As Jesus points out about pagan prayers, we cannot allow our insecurity to result in verbal self-absorption. God can't get a word in because we're controlling the

1. Hall, *When You Pray*, 49.

conversation. In its healthiest form, this manner of praying is a communal experience, where we lift up to God our questions: about life, love, and justice. It's not that God needs to be reminded of the needs of this world. We need to hear the message again. We list the names of those peoples and countries that are at war, captive to violence and hatred, and in so doing, we are both recognizing the pain of this world—the pain of God, if you will—and we are committing ourselves to be God's hands of healing and wholeness. So, the conversational prayer becomes a verbal rededication to love the world God loves and calls us to be our Maker's agents in the history of justice-making. But conversations are very well and good. If I am trapped in a burning building, you can bet I am not going to pray a conversation with God, waiting for my Creator's response. No. When I am desperate, I will cry out for help. And this is the final major form of prayer: the cry for help.

Prayer as a Wish List

When I was four, I wanted a blue dump truck. I plagued my parents night and day with my need for a blue dump truck. There was no doubt in my infant mind what it must look like—a playful baby blue with a lift lever to dump the load, a plastic windshield, and doors that opened. Large enough not to roll under my low bed and small enough to ride on the back of my tricycle. How did I get that image in my head? No matter. The toy truck was real and I required it. Don't talk to me about oxygen! I didn't need it in the same way that I needed that truck.

So, I would pester my parents. As Christmas approached, I increased my assault on their defenses. Any Santa Claus that was unfortunate enough to hoist me up onto his lap would get my litany of reasons why this truck would fulfill my every desire.

Prayer can be like that. Sure, that's a rather crass comparison, but the dynamics are the same. We approach the Almighty's throne with a list of requests—some are trivial like toy trucks, others much more serious: freedom from the cancer that is eating away our health, healing for a father whose heart is declining. Some are parochial, like a plea for the local church community's well-being. Some are world-transforming: peace in the Middle East and justice for the destitute. Some are heart-wrenching: the safe return of a soldier from battle or a second chance for a child struck by leukemia.

Then come the personal trials. We pray to God and ask for direction in a life gone off the rails or for a job when we are unemployed. As the prayer list goes up from lower-level desires to the higher ones, our words become more clipped, edged with simple desperation. We cry out to God in monosyllabic anguish, sighs and deep silences that are pure supplication.Now, it is quite easy to cast stones at what appears to be a one-sided relationship with God. Is that the level to which we are reduced? Self-absorbed little children pleading with a heavenly Parent? Surely, we must rise above this immature practice of prayer as a wish list!

There are good reasons to suggest that prayer as pure petition is unhelpful. First, it tends to create dependency and immaturity among believers. We won't or can't grow up if all we play a child/parent game. We expect God to fix our problems, to produce blue toy trucks out of thin air. If we only treat God like a mother who will kiss our cuts to make them better, we may never leave the nursery room of life. Every prick and pinch of growing will dismay us, and we will not have tools with which to confront the complicated breakdowns that plague every human life.

The second problem flows directly from the first: When we are trapped in a kindergarten faith, we don't have a well-developed response ability. We can't understand how to move our anguish into action, and it becomes difficult to look beyond our own personal problems. The difficulty with unrelenting self-absorption is that it is so persistent. Keep in mind the frustration we have with our teenagers and how they can't seem to see beyond their noses to respond to the call for compassion coming from people and events around them. That's how our Mother in heaven must feel when our praying seriously confuses her with Santa Claus. Not helpful. Not pretty.

But these criticisms are disingenuous. When we are not caught on the horns of life's dilemmas, it can feel self-righteous. But bring us to the brink of the abyss, and we will all quite naturally revert to a singular plea for assurance and assistance from our God who is like an Almighty Father. It's natural. It's how we're made. Augustine explained this prayerful reflex. He said that our hearts were shaped by God, and so it is natural that we return to our maker in times of trouble: "Our hearts are restless until they find rest in thee."[2]

Let us not be ashamed of our pleading. Quite frankly, there are moments when the chaos *is* overwhelming. I love the T-shirt slogan: "If you can keep your head while all those around you are losing theirs, you don't

---

2. Augustine of Hippo, *The Confessions of St. Augustine*, 1.

understand the problem." So, when disaster strikes, we boldly ask for God's help.

Even when things do not change, this prayer wish list is essential because it becomes a vehicle for our pent-up fears and frustrations. We have to cry out. Imagine when a child's fever rises beyond the breaking point. What mother does not cry out to heaven? What else is left? Sometimes it's an angry fist-shaking, more often it is a weeping plea for something, anything that looks like hope.

Our Praying: Metaphorical Language

There is an implicit order in these three forms of prayer, a natural progression that occurs when we grow in faith. We move through the wish list to a space where the encounter with God is more like a conversation, until there comes a time when words are no longer necessary. At that stage, we do not need to express anything, but simply to rest in peace in God.

However, there are circumstances that will invite us from the sacredness of this wordless communion with God. When calamity strikes, who doesn't return again to a wish list style of prayer? Likewise, when we are struggling with a life decision or searching for hope in the midst of darkness, it is quite appropriate to use prayer as a way to think our way into the presence of God.

So, there is no right or wrong place from which to pray as long as we don't get exclusively stuck in one form of prayer over all others.

A final word.

This prayer language is all metaphorical. Let us never lose sight of the fact that we are speaking to a mystery that exists beyond our words and above our understanding. To assume that our few words and titles, like "Father" or "God" or "Lord," capture the entity we are addressing is very foolish. It's as if an ant, riding on the back of an elephant, declares himself to be in charge of the animal beneath.

All our words are metaphors. The original crafters of our most famous prayers understood this. God is not literally "our Father." It is better to say that God is *like* "our Father." Our praying is relational and so it is entirely appropriate to name the "Other" as a parent, friend, or master. These are all nouns that assume relationship, but let us never make the mistake that God is somehow circumscribed by these words. God's mystery is well beyond our vocabulary and it is essential to remember always that we only approach the Maker of the Universe with feeble comparisons.

Currently, it has been fashionable in church circles to argue over the gender of God. One side asserts that the masculine language of the Scriptures must be followed. The other suggests that we need to expand our vocabulary, enlisting the many layers of gendering that are possible to us. God is "she." So is the Spirit. Inclusive language has become the mark of a faithfulness of the liberal church just as "God the Father" is the bulwark of fundamentalist belief. While I have lost interest in the fires of this particular battle, the debate is important, as it illustrates to everyone that all of our names for God are metaphors—none is eternally true or heaven-mandated. As the human condition evolves, so will our images of God.

Jesus chose to call his Creator a "father," to lead his followers into an intimate and close relationship with God. My concluding point is that the original community was not torn by our current debate. They were not worried if God was "literally" their heavenly Father or simply a metaphorical, parent-like being. The distinction between literalism and metaphorical language was not the issue, and it raises questions that distract us from the real problem of biblical language. The chief concern was *meaning*.

What did the first audience really *mean* by reciting the "Our Father"?

Surely it was a simple assertion. God is close, loves us with the compassion of a parent. Our mothers and fathers are those unique beings. We all have one or the other or both who know us so well. They've seen us grow, witnessed our nobility, and watched us make horrendous mistakes. They know us, all too well. We can't pretend when it comes to our parents. Yet it is an irrefutable fact that our mothers and fathers, whether on earth or in heaven, nevertheless love us most!

That is the foundation of our praying: A God who knows us from our rising up to our falling down (Ps 139) still wants us to know that we are loved, without condition and without limit.

3

Starting in the Middle:
"Thy Kingdom Come"

Getting the Game Plan:

Do you like football? Know how it works?

Even if it's not your favorite game, you've probably seen a game or two. While you can live in North America without actually viewing an entire Sunday afternoon football match, even the most uninterested would know the rudiments of the sport, having seen allusions to the basics of football in beer commercials or first-run movies.

So, football.

Join with me in a fiction. Fast forward to several millennia from now and imagine that the sport of football has disappeared entirely, along with rule books, video footage, and team rosters. Not a trace is left. All collective memory has been wiped clean. You'd be surprised how few generations that takes! Then, through a surprise discovery of a playing field, archeologists reconstruct the "ancient" game of football. These scientists present their findings to the Third Annual Association of Ancient Sports held in 5011. What would that report sound like? How would they explain football by what they uncovered in their big dig?

Perhaps something like this:

> *Friends, we are so pleased today to present our findings, the results of extensive research on site 3756 of the ancient city of Green Bay—a large city found on what was once an immense inland lake, situated*

in the northern sector of a state called Wisconsin, part of the original American empire of the twenty-first century.

Site 3756 offers up a great mystery, one which will require extensive research on the part of this society and others as we reconstruct a sacred religious ritual we believe was known as "football." Given the size of the sanctuary temple we have uncovered, our initial assumptions are that this ritual religion must have enjoyed considerable popularity in that period. While we have only uncovered a small portion of the temple complex, our estimates would suggest that between 50,000 to 80,000 individuals could have seated themselves in this open-air amphitheatre.

Currently, we have found only a few artifacts that were buried under some of the crumbling walls of the stadium (including strange, cheese-shaped headgear), but we believe we have sufficient evidence to begin to make some statements about this popular twenty-first–century pigskin ritual.

First, football appears to be an ancient marching, processional religion in which teams of professional acolytes/ warriors would take to a central field and perform elaborate marches for the enjoyment of the audience and the adoration of the pigskin deity.[1] The holy field was marked off in yards, an antiquated standard of measurement equivalent to a little under a meter. The field and the markers suggest a competitive nature to these holy marches. Perhaps, each team of acolytes was vying for a favored position in what may have been more elaborate ceremonies held on a high holy day.

There have been suggestions, given the recent discovery of two spears joined by a chain, that football involved some form of javelin tossing. The chain is exactly ten yards long and it may well be that the two teams needed these sticks for markers.

Each team of acolytes wore bright colors, so that marching teams would never mistake one another. We have no idea how many times these teams of acolytes/warriors would process past each other, but given the food production equipment we unearthed in the west sector of one portion of the stadium, we estimate that such marching ritual must have lasted for days, if not weeks.

We are fully aware of the manuscript that another team from this society uncovered. Classified as Codex GB2045, much about this document is still inconclusive. But it is quite suggestive . . . showing us a series of marching prescribed rites that a team of acolytes might perform for the pigskin deity (rites with quite suggestive names): "the

---

1. *It appears that this pigskin God was never named or addressed directly, no doubt in deference to the holiness of the God's name. But a monogram NFL is often used as a discrete substitute for the God's name.*

Hail Mary," "the Screen," "the Reverse," "the Statue of Liberty." There is even one called "the Give and Go." We are not in a position to make conclusive comment on this manuscript except to suggest that we have uncovered the secrets of the marching teams' strategies to out-perform the other.

However, let us not be distracted by these colorful manuscript interpretations. There appears to be little doubt that site 3756 offers conclusive evidence that the central point of these elaborate rituals was to escort a sacred pigskin ball from one end of the field to another. This appears to be the entire focus of this ancient rite. So holy is the pigskin ball that only certain holy warriors could touch and carry it across the holy lines on the sanctuary field . . .

Well, that's enough.

You get the picture.

It would be quite possible to draw the entirely wrong conclusions about a forgotten human activity, even though we have all the facts in front of us. If we had never seen a game of football or heard someone explain it and why it is played, we could get the whole thing upside down. The source of excitement and the final purpose of the sport would be lost to us. It would be difficult to distinguish between the peripheral dimensions and the central ones. And in so doing we might miss the entire point of football. Even with the facts laid out logically, if there is no one to tell us which is the primary point and which are secondary points, we are lost. Errors are almost certain.

What if the Prayer poses a similar problem? Isn't it possible that we have been using this prayer under false pretenses?

There are two series of questions I will ask to help focus this dilemma. First, we have to ask about the guiding principle behind the Prayer. What's its chief point? What did it mean to the original audience? When they gathered in a circle and began the "Our Father," what did they think they were doing? For this chapter, we will focus on a second question, that of emphasis. Where would I place the accent in this prayer? Which of the phrases is most important? Is there one of the petitions in the Prayer that acts as the actual beginning? Picture a circle of disciples praying the "Our Father." Where did those first voices put their energy?

We Begin with Humility

As I mentioned in the last chapter, the Prayer begins with a spirit of humility and so must we.

I am well aware of the danger of injecting back into the first-century matrix a very twenty-first–century idea. That is always the challenge when facing those who would travel back to the initial steps and stages of the movement of the carpenter from Nazareth. The quest for the historical Jesus, which is well over 200 years old, is fraught with examples of just such an intrusion. We have at one time turned Jesus into a Victorian gentleman reclining stoically on his cross. More recently, he appears as a Marxist Latin American revolutionary bent on social reform.

We step into this question of the original intention of the Prayer with considerable caution and humility. It will be impossible to avoid entirely the distortions that are invisible to us, but the simple awareness that we have them may temper our zeal for making closed pronouncements. Perhaps if we identify a few more dominant biases, we will evade the more obvious misinterpretations. I can see three major "distractions" of the twenty-first century which have no place in the first century. The first two I have alluded to already; the final point raises what I consider to be our primary concern when we approach the gospels.

Distractions of the Twenty-First–Century Historicity

First, we often come to Scripture with post-Enlightenment questions, assuming that what confounds us would quite naturally do the same for the first company of Jesus. For instance, we consider that the corroboration between historical veracity and spiritual truth is essential. In order for something to be true it must have actually happened in time and space. Seeing is believing. Taking off from the example of Thomas, we might be tempted to argue that the disciples spent endless hours arguing about how Jesus actually performed his miracles and whether it was possible for a simple man to reflect the power of God. How do you actually bring a dead person, like Lazarus, back to life? But these are modern questions. In the first century, the equation is reversed: believing is seeing.

No one is asking Jesus if he could really calm the waters, or how he cured the lepers or indeed if rising from the dead is truly possible. And quite clearly even his critics were not perplexed by Jesus' actions, trying to distinguish between historical and metaphorical truth. They naturally assumed that someone could commune with the Creator of the universe and transform the material world through this connection. They never asked if Jesus was capable of seemingly impossible feats of healing and hospitality—they took this as a given. Their question was never whether Jesus had miraculous power, but *whose* power he used: God's or the devil's.

Likewise, the first-century Hebraic mind did not separate the material from the spiritual world; they were one. The dualism of the Hellenistic, gentile world was foreign to the Jewish community. It's not that they didn't know about the very attractive and practical distinction between body and soul; they just didn't believe it.

In this case, our challenge will be to suspend our desire to separate verifiable fact from unsupportable or superstitious events. Rather, we should continue to focus on the question of meaning. It isn't fruitful to ask about what really happened, but to explore what an action, story, or parable might have meant.

Individuality

A second distraction. We might be tempted to portray Jesus as a democrat—well before such a term was coined. There is little doubt that we would like him to reflect a sensitivity to human liberties and the need for personal expression. Surely, the prince of peace would uphold a charter of rights and freedoms and defend the claims of individual emancipation. Alas, this may be a desirable picture, but it has little place in the social and political matrix of the first century.

Of course, there is considerable evidence in the Gospels that Jesus was sympathetic to personal problems. For instance, he was constantly confronting the false and often damaging correlation between disease and sin, the prejudice against women and other untouchables. However, it would be a distortion to assume that he advocated individual human rights. Jesus did not use these categories to describe his movement, even though the end result may appear to be very close to what we consider to be the foundations of a modern democracy.

In his world, there was no assumption of personal power or individual agency. Walk back to the first century, and you enter a world of the corporate personality. In a society based on patronage, the singular human being was always subsumed under the patriarch and clan. If the chief is well, I am too. His honor is my honor. It's my responsibility to participate in the collective life of the community and I do not assume I have a personal life separate from the life of the whole. It is my job to reinforce the power and influence of my patriarch and so increase the social and political capacity of the whole community.

Likewise, there was no expectation of immediate or direct access to power. Agency, the capacity to get something done, was vested in the hierarchical system of interconnecting favors. It was the overlord's job to achieve results. Whether we speak of the palace or the temple, one did not assume one could or even should control the decision-making process. It was the monarch, high priest, or head of the household who was given the responsibility of, as our world would put it, producing outcomes. One influenced these "can-do" people only through a mediator or patron. Power was always mediated.

This point is a challenge to understand. Why not try a little experiment? Look at your cell phone and ask yourself how close you could get to your country's source of power. Could you reach the White House? How far up the chain of command could you go before you would get a polite refusal? We might get past the first layer of receptionists. Perhaps if we had a name of a presidential functionary we could reach a bit higher. The notion of actually trying to do it—to speak to the President—is not too outlandish. In Canada, for instance, it is entirely within the realm of possibility that a private citizen could speak with the head of state.

No matter the country, the potential of immediate and direct access is in your hand! The cell phone is based on an assumption that everyone has the right to speak to anyone else. Give me a network, and I can touch the world. Such an idea is an anathema in the world of Jesus. Never gonna happen!

Riches

One final distraction coming from the twenty-first–century perspective is riches. We are most confounded by the fact of first-century scarcity. Rich Christians will have difficulty embracing and understanding the nature of the gospel story because they have been hypnotized into a kind of intellectual and spiritual lethargy. We have too much! With the passing of a generation who went through the Great Depression, most North American Christians do not have any firsthand experience of desperation or need.

Our next meal is never in doubt. We take an unbelievable level of abundance for granted.

During the time of the Reformation, a follower of Martin Luther named Karlstadt went about the countryside with a Latin translation of the Bible, and he would enter into the hovels of poor peasants and ask them to translate it for him. He knew that it was only when the words were spoken out of the context of poverty that they made any sense.

A radical and often fruitless gesture, perhaps, but Karlstadt's instincts were correct. The good news of Jesus was framed by want, refined by desperation, and preached into scarcity. Rich Christians quite naturally "spiritualize" the ideas, turning obviously material statements into metaphysical ones. For instance, Luke offers the first of the Beatitudes as "Blessed are the poor, for theirs is the kingdom of God" (Luke 6:20), a declaration that those who live with the conditions of material deprivation will soon enjoy the tangible benefits of God's justice. A very clear statement about the here and now of hunger. Matthew adds a spiritual codicil to Luke: "Blessed are the poor *in spirit* for theirs is the kingdom of heaven" (Matt 5:3).[2] Now we're talking about a realm at arm's length from the daily grind of survival. I doubt if Matthew expected his listeners to place God's reign in a world above and beyond history, but he certainly diminishes Luke's emphasis on the actual conditions of poverty by adding the words "in spirit."

We who have enjoyed material well-being appreciate Matthew's focus because it corresponds to our frame of reference. Our hunger pangs afflict the soul, not the stomach. It's not that we are entirely insensitive to the claims of the vulnerable and marginalized; it is simply a question of our context and needs. When tonight's dinner is in the fridge, I have the luxury of contemplating my spiritual yearnings and therefore I hear the words of Jesus in a different light.

So, those who enjoy abundance can and will quite naturally find the words of Jesus to be examples of tremendous spiritual importance. His

2. At this juncture, be careful not to be distracted by Matthew's use of the word "heaven" when speaking of the reign of God. "Kingdom of heaven" is exactly the same as kingdom of God. Matthew avoids what he considers an unholy direct reference to God by substituting the word *heaven*, but it means the same thing. As Crossan points out in the introduction to his speeches on the "kingdom of God," it is equivalent to speaking of the "White House" instead of the "president." For example, when an announcer says, "the White House" took a position or made a pronouncement, the audience knows it is not the building itself but the person who occupies the building who is speaking. Likewise, for Matthew, it is not heaven but one who rules in heaven who will establish a "kingdom." For further reading consult Crossan, *God and Empire*.

parables and healing miracles point to profound archetypal truths that have survived generations of philosophical debate and spoken to profound spiritual anxiety.

Let us never fall into the trap of reverse self-righteous interpretation. It is fruitless to argue that a perspective shaped by affluence is inappropriate or distorted. However, there can be no doubt that the initial words of Jesus were oriented by and for the mundane, not the esoteric. His stories spoke initially to the daily grind of making a living, feeding a family, and surviving the disastrous conditions of an occupied territory. And it is in the crucible of those basic struggles that his words caught fire and transformed the here and now of human history. Heaven comes later. In fact, it was 300 years after the sermons of Jesus were first preached that the Roman Empire embraced Christianity and began to blunt his more radical political edges with spiritual addenda.

My point here is quite simple: rich Christians have a difficult time hearing the good news. This is not a reason to give up in despair or abandon the "kingdom of God project." Rather, it is our simple truth. Wealth muffles the cries of the gospel and our first task is to get the wax out of our ears, so to speak. Let us remove as many obstacles to hearing Christ's words as possible. For sure, the barrier of riches is a serious problem that even Jesus recognized (Mark 10:25). He made a joke about camels and needles to soften our dismay and to reinforce his point that even when some things seem humanly impossible, God achieves miracles. Let us proceed, trusting in that same God to guide us beyond our own doubts.

Keeping these three cautionary notes about modern distractions in mind and proceeding in a spirit of humility, we can now ask our question: Where does the Prayer begin?

Where the Prayer Does Not Begin

If we are to find the central focus or motivation of the Prayer, it is necessary to ask a much thornier question. What is the key, directing message of Jesus? Is there a single phrase that captures his mission, an idea that would quite naturally direct our understanding of his prayer? Allow me to answer that question by focusing on where I believe the Prayer does *not* begin.

Some might summarize the faith this way: "Jesus is Lord and Savior." There! We're done. However, contrary to popular belief, Jesus did not direct attention to himself or his supposed messiahship. Of course, in John's

Gospel he claims to be the "way, the truth and the life" (John 14:6) and embraces the title of messiahship when it is offered, but the fourth Gospel is at least five generations away from the historical events it describes, and therefore it often reflects second-century theology much more than first-century reality.

If we accept scholarly consensus, Mark is the earliest narrative account of the ministry of Jesus. In this first Gospel, Jesus is often portrayed as deflecting any attention on his person or potential messiahship. He quite often silences those who would proclaim his glory or praise his heaven-sent power. At times, he can be downright rude[3] in silencing the evil spirits who are most vocal in their awareness of Jesus' monarchial heritage and divine destiny.

Likewise, it seems evident that the constant moving from town to town undermines any attempt Jesus might have made to establish a home base. He was clearly embraced as a spiritual patron. The people recognized his teaching as having a new "authority" (Mark 1:21, 27), but he did not settle down long enough for the disciples to build the proper hierarchical structures of influence—as would have been expected by any self-respecting company following a spiritual leader.

Peter and others try to act as Jesus' gatekeepers. They restrict access to their leader, quite naturally reinforcing the social norms of the day. You didn't just walk up to this new leader and ask for a favor. You had to go through his closest lieutenants. Noisy children and pesky mothers are a particular problem they tried to control (Mark 10:13), and we know that didn't last long. Jesus would not allow himself to be "handled" in that fashion. He seems to have taken pains to be directly accessible to the lowest and the most untouchable of his world. He was not a distant Lord.

While Jesus did undertake an itinerant preaching mission, it would be a mistake to compare him to recent evangelistic extravaganzas in which people are invited to embrace Jesus as their "Savior." This may be a message we want to promote as Christians, but it has no place in first-century Palestine. He heals lepers and sends them way to seek approval from their own spiritual leaders (Mark 1:44). Those who are touched by his healing want to join him, but Jesus often tells them to go their way and say nothing about what had happened (Mark 10:52, 1:44). Perhaps there is no better rebuff

---

3. A man is possessed by an evil spirit who shouts out that he knows who Jesus is: "the Holy man of God." And Jesus in response to this proclamation of messiahship "yelled at it and said, 'Shut up and get out of him.'" (Mark 1:25)

of his "savior-ship" role than his curt reply to the rich man who wanted to praise him (Mark 10:17). "Good master," he began, and Jesus interrupted the question by deflecting this bit of flattery with, "Why do you call me 'good?' There is none good but God."

On a deeper level, modern Christians might raise the claims of the cross and reply that Jesus' gift to the world was his death at Golgotha. It was there that he "bought" our souls. Through his sacrifice, we who were lost are saved. Most commonly we hear that he "died" for our sins and that is the guiding fact of his life and ministry. If we are to understand the Prayer, it can only be through the lens of his sacrifice. In technical terms this position is called "substitutionary" atonement and it was given classic expression by Anselm of Canterbury in the twelfth century. In a nutshell, this theory assumes that human beings are beyond redemption and weighed down by an impossible weight of sin. They have no ability to make amends with their God, who is both just and righteous. Because of God's justice, the debt of sin we owe cannot simply be wiped out. Someone must pay, and Jesus is the solution. God "substitutes" his unlimited merit (gained through his innocent death on the cross) for our unwieldy debt. We are saved! Hallelujah.

On the basis of this theory, it could be argued that the central vocation of Jesus' life was his death. Apart from turning the entire Galilean ministry into a meaningless "warm up act," this approach to the Christian story poses two serious problems, both embedded in substitutionary atonement.

First, it assumes twisted intentionality on God's part. Given God's all-knowing, all-seeing character, the idea of a necessary sacrifice seems both sick and sadistic. Crossan[4] uses the image of a firefighter saving a child from a burning building. In the process, this hero loses his life and the newspapers praise him for his sacrifice. And indeed, his saving actions are made holy[5] for he offers up his life to restore life to a child. It's a story from which legends are built. But imagine what it would do to our image of God if we were to imply that the fireman's death was necessary. Seeing the fire and the desperation of the child, God says, "Someone must die today. If not the kid, we'll kill the firefighter." This makes no sense, even given some potential for culpability on the part of the child. The firefighter was acting in good faith. What kind of God are we worshipping when innocent people must be made to suffer death? So, the first problem with substitutionary

---

4. Crossan, *God and Empire*, 140.

5. The Latin roots of the word are "*sacra*" or holy, and "*facere*," to do or make. "Sacrifice" literally means "to make holy."

atonement is that it turns God into a vindictive deity whose justice is always retributive. While such a punishing God can be found in Scripture, it is not the dominant portrait of the God of the people.

The second problem with this particular theory is that it cuts through the nerve of human responsibility. When the entire ministry of Jesus is regarded as the pre-game show to the real event of the cross, we are not invited to take our time on earth with any measure of seriousness. It's heaven where the good things wait for us. Moreover, the basis of substitutionary thinking is that we are basically helpless, hapless creatures who require God to do a deal with Jesus. Human beings are excluded from any participation in their own salvation.

This kind of distance between God and humanity makes sense in a world where our anxiety over condemnation is a dominant theme. When we are so burdened by our guilt that we require an outside being to absolve and forgive us, substitutionary atonement works well because it takes human pain seriously. However, in an era when, as the German theologian martyr Dietrich Bonhoeffer suggested[6] "the world has come of age," it will be disastrous to undermine humanity's ethical agency. Benign no longer, we are now too destructive as a species to be left out of the plans and purposes for our own or the world's salvation.

It is for these reasons that I mistrust any proposal to make "Jesus died for my sins" the focal point for the Christian movement. Finding the central orienting principle to the Jesus event is not as easy as we might have imagined.

If Jesus did not preach about himself as God's chosen one or present himself as the answer to our deepest questions, perhaps we could say that his message was about conversion. The focal point of his ministry was repentance. Wasn't he called a prophet? Couldn't we say that his mission was directed by the ancient and revered practice of turning the people's hearts back toward God?

Speaking of repentance raises the possibility of applying an historical test to our exploration into the guiding motivation of the Jesus movement. We can compare Jesus to his closest colleague: John the Baptizer. If we are to understand Jesus' central purpose, we can contrast what Jesus says and does against the method of John. In that comparison, we will recognize the importance of the singular idea in Jesus' message: "the kingdom of God."

---

6. Bonhoeffer, *Letters and Papers from Prison*, 178.

John and Symbolic Nonviolent Action

Most Christians picture John as a wild-eyed desert hermit who performed regular baptisms in the Jordan River. Isn't it a first-century version of the initiation rituals we experience in our modern churches? People came forward individually to receive his prayers and allowed themselves to be immersed in the water. Repenting of their sins, each person went down under the waves, dying to the old self. They rose from the water as renewed and recreated children of God.

Certainly, John's intention appears to have been to purify Israel. This rejuvenated people would be the foundation upon which God would restore the fortunes of the ancient kingdom of David. God would bring justice to the earth when the people turned away from their false or shallow faith.

It is possible to see how such a mass movement would disturb religious authorities and the local political elite. Tyrants hate crowds because they are uncontrollable. Often people discover their courage to resist oppression when they gather into a mob, a courage that eludes them as individuals. Any inspired and fervent crowd would attract attention and a wise ruler would seek to quell it quickly. So, John is imprisoned and the movement apparently withered away after a generation.

I wouldn't discount this interpretation, but what if we pushed the historical record a little further? An axiom for Bible study that I have often used goes something like this: "Read the Gospels well, but keep your eyes on the ground." The words are important, but so is the geography. I can think of no better way to explain John the Baptizer and his movement apart from following the symbolism and meaning found in the landscape that is the backdrop to his preaching and acting.

Ask yourself, "Where does John come from?"

Easy answer. He lives in the desert.

Right. And who else lives in the desert? Isn't that where God dwells? The people survived in the wilderness for forty years, communing directly with God, relying upon their Maker; trusting their God for everything including bread. The desert is where miracles of trust take place. Like countless calls to "move back to the land" in the last century, it held out a promise of hope—like coming home to the way things should be.

John invites his community back into this respected, reverent, dangerous place. There they are asked to reevaluate their lives and loves. Having been convinced that a new way of life is required, what do they do? As a people, they cross over the river into the promised land, moving east to west.

Isn't this a version of symbolic, nonviolent action? The people of God re-enter the promised land to reclaim it. Marching as their ancestors had, from the wilderness into a land filled with milk and honey, they remind themselves and their rulers—even the Romans—of who they are and to whom they belong. John and his followers may have believed that this symbolic action was sufficient unto itself; it alone would inspire God to act. Kick-starting God's revolution into top gear, so to speak. Or perhaps John had more concrete plans in mind. Did he expect his converts to coalesce into a spiritually emboldened military force? We will never know John's final ambitions because he was cut down too quickly.

Of course, on the surface, symbolic action appears quite impotent. But a modern example illustrates that such types of symbols have considerable power to galvanize the people against what is considered to be unjust rule. The collection of people opposed to President Obama called their movement "the Tea Party," and by making reference to the original event that arguably began the American Revolution, they clothed their political program in patriotism. At the same time, they made a very strong connection between their resistance to medical reforms and the patriots' rejection of unfair taxation. Potent stuff!

I imagine that Roman rulers were just as intelligent and wary as any other organized occupying force. They could read the signs. John was play-acting a war of restoration and independence. The first time he leads a group of zealous converts across the Jordan, one might laugh it off as foolish. But as the crowds grow, and more and more eager feet splash across the river expecting a new world to appear, you cannot ignore the implications of John's ministry.

It is not surprising that John was dispatched. It was just a matter of time. The rulers, both Roman and Jewish, read the signs of the times well. They knew if they imprisoned John, the baptizing movement would die, and it did.

The Kingdom of God

There is no question that Jesus had personally participated in John's mission—whatever it might have been. Either as personal call to repentance or a collective symbolic act, he witnessed its failure firsthand. Jesus was sympathetic to John and never denies his importance, but quite clearly, he initiates his ministry in Galilee, preaching a different approach to the good news. At the beginning of Mark's gospel, we read: "After John was locked up, Jesus came to Galilee proclaiming God's good news. His message went, 'The time is up. God's imperial rule is closing in. Change your ways and put your trust in the good news'" (Mark 1:14–15).[7]

In most translations, Jesus calls his mission "the kingdom of God." Whether it is present among us now or coming soon, the *basilea tou theou*[8] appears to be Jesus' central and singular description of what believers can expect. Almost all his healing stories and parables are a function of describing how and why this kingdom of God is important and immanent.

In chapter seven, we will examine the material and social content of this concept. For the present, let us simply recognize that Jesus appears to have lived out his kingdom of God in a way distinct from John. He learned from the baptizer that it is essential to embody ideas in more than symbolic action—preaching is not enough. Symbolic action is very suggestive but it also falls short. Truth must be a lived out, not as distant hope, but as daily reality.

In contrast to John's overt political action, Jesus incorporates the kingdom of God in two more domestic activities: hospitality and healing. Wherever he goes, he feasts with the hungry, heals the sick, and then proclaims that God's kingdom has come close.

If we take the sending out of the disciples as a paradigm of his mission, the pattern is made explicit. Let's hear the gospel story from Luke 9:1–6:

> He called the twelve together and gave them power and authority over evil demons and to heal diseases. He sent them out to announce God's imperial rule and to heal the sick. He said to them, "Don't take anything for the road: neither staff nor knapsack, neither bread nor money; no one is to take two shirts. And whichever house you enter, stay there and leave from there. And wherever

---

7. This translation is taken from the scholar's version found in *The Complete Gospels*. This version is the result of collaboration of the Jesus seminar and will be used throughout this text as the primary version for gospel citations. Any other translation will be noted by added abbreviations after biblical citations: e.g., NRSV.

8. Let us be clear that the original phrase in Greek is patriarchal. There is no way to avoid the fact that a *basilea* is ruled by a king. It would be a mistake to turn this word into the "kin-dom" of God to avoid the patriarchal and hierarchal connotations of the "kingdom." For in so doing, we rob the concept of both its concrete historical relevancy and its ethical agency. Jesus intended for his movement to be a recognizable and authentic organization that had the social legitimacy and political authority to act.

they do not welcome you, leave the town and shake the dust from your feet in witness against them." And they set out and went from village to village, bringing good news and healing everywhere.

There are a number of key ideas to note in this description of a travelling kingdom. First, the disciples were to travel light. Without a knapsack, there could be no begging. Kingdom workers do not panhandle or hustle their meals. Not taking a staff signaled a willing vulnerability on the journey, since the staff was more than a mere walking stick. It was your first line of defense, a simple yet effective weapon. No extra shirts or sandals reinforces the picture of a mendicant strategy. No one comes prepared to defend or feed themselves. The plan is disarmingly simple: you arrive in a local village having to trust in their hospitality. In fact, that was essential, since you needed them to want to offer food. The disciples healed, and in return they were fed. The kingdom of God, when it comes to town, is not a show of power nor is it a free ride. It invites reciprocity. This image is underlined in the admonition not to go from house to house. You stay where you have been invited, rather than traveling to bigger and better banquet halls. You're not in the "Jesus business" for self-gratification or aggrandizement. The whole point is to allow for each side to have an offering: the townsfolk have food and an open table. The disciples have healing power and an open heart. Clearly, in that miraculous mixture of mutuality, God's reign comes to earth.

Apparently, this incarnation of the kingdom of God actually happened often. The disciples reported that they actually did it: healed the people, received their hospitality in return. A knock at the door of a peasant's hovel and the world was changed. I can imagine that once begun, this open hospitality and healing spread rapidly from village to village. Even without the presence of Jesus or the disciples, the people discovered the power of shared burdens and a common meal. No one went hungry and none was left out. Talk about miracles!

However, the disciples are sent out to villages not to establish themselves in a specific locality, but to embody God's reign and then move on. Each day one is to incarnate God's reign from the beginning. No temple building, no cult following, no "Jesus groupies." The kingdom of God is built on hospitality and healing that takes to the open road so that none allows themselves to fall into a pattern of patronage. The entire point of his approach is to inspire responsibility and co-creativity in the coming of God's reign on earth—a lesson that might well be reshaped for the modern church.

We would do well to keep this passage from Luke in our minds as Christ's best example of the kingdom of God. It underlines a number of often essential characteristics of this mission. First, God's reign is not for another time or place. It has been tempting, especially given Matthew's use of the term *kingdom of heaven*, to see this realm above and beyond human existence. But clearly all the Gospel writers reflect Christ's intent that the kingdom of God be part of this world.

The term *kingdom* is both practical and legitimate. Jesus uses it intentionally to speak of a reign of God that is both understandable and legitimate in the eyes of his audience. In that time, a kingdom was what you needed to get something done. The audience who first heard the phrase would not be offended either by the monarchial overtones nor the assumption of a masculine deity. Their focus would have been on the very intriguing idea that God could be an earthly ruler. In their ears the "kingdom of God" translates in this fashion: what would the world look like if God were made king? In our time, we might translate the idea in a slightly different fashion. "How would our country be different if God were elected president or prime minister?" By employing this term to capture the essence of his movement, Jesus is drawing all ears and eyes back down to earth. No heaven-bent gazes, no flights of spirit yearning. Jesus' mission is all about God's love and transformation of this earthly realm. As John's gospel puts it, "For God so loved the world . . ." (John 3:16).

In the second place, the kingdom of God was not a fanciful idea or list of theoretical propositions. It would have been an intriguing enough concept as a philosophy alone. But that was not enough for Jesus. His concept had to be lived out. Each day, he rose to recreate this reign of God in the midst of the people. As mentioned above, the disciples were trained to make this kingdom of God come alive among the people. It was on the basis of a lively and obviously engaging reality that the kingdom movement spread through Galilee and beyond.

Finally, it should be noted that the kingdom of God was not a benign communal impulse. Of course, it had the advantage of grouping people together and empowering them to create their own sense of food security and social well-being.[9] Nevertheless, the creation of cohesive self-sustaining communities has a political dimension that cannot be ignored.

Imagine if a group of American citizens were to preach "Jesus is our President," and to believe it. Not just as a theoretical possibility or spiritual

9. For a more extensive explanation of these two points, see chapters seven and eight.

symbol. What if they lived as if Jesus was their sole and authoritative leader? Picture this group living in such a way as to make the secular presidency irrelevant. Can you imagine that the actual President would not take notice? Caesar was no less intelligent and sensitive to alternate political systems and divided loyalties.

Put bluntly, a movement described as "the kingdom of God" was nothing if it not political.

Clearly this kingdom was not a typical monarchy. According to Jesus it was characterized by children (Mark 10:14). Modern sentimentality turns this notion into a description of childlike innocence, but it seems more likely that Jesus intended to contrast the presumed power and importance of the adults of his day with the clear disregard his society held for children. The kingdom of God is not about reinforcing the stereotypes of power. Rather, it lifted up the lowly and forgotten—even kids.

We Begin with the Kingdom

With all these qualifications taken into account, I would conclude with the simple affirmation that the Prayer begins and ends with the clear declaration of the kingdom of God. If you would know where Christ places his emphasis in this prayer we have recited for generations, it is on the phrase, "Thy kingdom come." Forget God's hallowed name—the Prayer gets into gear with the bold affirmation of a new world being established. In fact, the Prayer is essentially the elaboration of both the content and potency of God's reign here on earth.

Take up this prayer and you are transported to a new world. Hang on to your hats, this is going to be quite a ride!

However, one must be watchful. To take up this prayer is not simply to wish for the establishment of an impossible dream in a distant time. The Prayer is all about God's kingdom coming right now, this instant. There is an immediacy in these sixty-eight words that has been lost to most modern ears.

To understand this essential quality, we must take time to explore an ancient way of speaking. Called "performative" language, it is a transformative and powerful way to understand spoken words, and it is to that subject that our next chapter turns.

4

Performative Language: "Thy Kingdom Come"

A Walk to the Front of the Church

How TIRED OUR JOKES can become. Come to one of my classes in religious studies, and you'll hear me introduce myself as a pastor of a church using what has become a very effective, but overused bit of humor. I confess, "I do marriages." Then to throw these young students off their well-worn prejudices, I add, "Anyone want to get married today? I have a special. Two for one."

They laugh, but I know this joke is getting tired—the punch line lacks the zest it once had.

All kidding notwithstanding, I do "do weddings" and it is only in that context that I understand the power of words and the potential they possess to change reality. Why don't you join me at front of the church for a moment and watch what happens?

First thing: the groom is nervous. His "best" man is whispering one-liners, bad jokes. Even though they were all bravado last night at the rehearsal, standing here now in the presence of their families (and God), they have clearly lost some of their machismo and they're covering up their fears with kidding. This moment is serious. I, for one, am thankful to see the deer-in-the-headlights anxiety in the eyes of the groom as the wedding march begins. He sees that his life is about to change radically.

Now, don't get distracted by the colors or shapes of gowns that are approaching you from the back. This is possibly the most unreal moment in a wedding! Most clergy will admit in the quiet of their studies that they have rarely seen a complete bridal procession that worked. Usually there is a sister or a cousin who should never have been forced to wear the uniform gown that the bride imposed. No, it is better to focus on the broad smiles of the attendants, the sober comportment of the maid of honor, and the deeply sincere glances between bride and groom as the white-gowned mirage floats into her place by the man of her dreams.

It is when these two hearts stand before me that I know I am blessed. What an honor to help two people celebrate their profound affection and enable them to build on that love and actualize a new existence! Can you feel it? There's a kind of sparkle in the air.

There are two individuals at the front, clearly wanting to commit themselves to one another. Let's take notice that they are not yet married. If the groom was to get cold feet, give in to his apprehensions, and walk back into my study, or if the bride were suddenly to act on all those doubts she was nursing while dressing in her mother's bedroom and run back down the aisle, well, it would be disappointing. Initially, there would be considerable shuffling of feet and embarrassed exchanges, shrugs of shoulders, or even quiet weeping. No doubt, the two families would feel some resentment. They would be left with quite awkward, pressing questions. What to do with a prearranged reception? How to explain to grandparents what has just *not* happened? Whether to return immediately the many cards and gifts piled up at the back of the church? Maybe one should wait till the dust has settled. If the two main participants in a wedding ended it right at the altar, it would be hard, but very soon people would begin to tell each other that "it was all for the best." Yes, it is much more important that people act with genuine sincerity. Even though there might be some brief hiccups, it is infinitely preferable never to marry than to get hitched under the wrong circumstances. How many marriages have taken place because everyone was caught up in the momentum of emotions, no one seriously questioning their long-term motivations? So, the bride and groom can part . . . even at the very last minute, and there are no lasting legal consequences. Do you agree?

But suppose that these two standing before us are not as quick off the mark as they should have been. They are both being carried along by the current of pre-wedding preparations, they let the ceremony proceed past the "I do" part, and they allow the minister to say the words, "By the power vested in me, I declare you to be husband and wife."

Well, now we have a problem if these two people want to separate. Before the "I do," it is a simple question of suffering emotional embarrassment. Post "I do" and it will now require a rank of lawyers and paperwork to cut the wedding ties. The spoken words "perform" what they say.

The words are spoken and change everything. I remind couples in the rehearsal that if I was to suffer a heart attack and collapse on the way to sign the marriage register, or if their marriage certificate were to spontaneously catch fire before they could put pen to paper, the wedding is nevertheless legal and binding. It is not the forms or the signatures that make a marriage a social contract. It is the spoken word that achieves that fact.

I'll say it again. The spoken words change everything.

Now I presume if we were to bring in a battery of investigative machines, we would discover that nothing has changed in the physiological or neurological makeup of each participant. Give them an MRI, subject them to blood tests or full body scans. Nothing is different from the moment before the words are spoken to the instant after the "I do." And yet everything is now new.

We're not simply speaking about the subjective perspective of the couple in question. Once the words are out in the air, everyone accepts that things are now different. We will now socialize with the man and women as an "authentic" couple. They will be naturally accredited with legitimacy because they are no longer "fooling around." Without question these two individuals will be accorded respect in the wider world—even among people who do not know them. They will enjoy privileges that hitherto would have been impossible. No sideways glances when they introduce each other to work colleagues or strangers. Marriage confers tangible security and "acceptability."

The entire wedding party, the gathered community, and the wider world know that everything has changed for these two people. Once the words are spoken, by common consent we all agree that a new reality has been created and we will accord this new reality both legal authority and social standing. No question.

The state of marriage created by our words is not temporary. The power of the words does not diminish with the passing of days (unlike my jokes). Quite the contrary. The longer the couple stays married, the stronger becomes the commonly held consensus that a new reality exists for these two people.

In summary, in marriage the spoken words have power to change reality. They bind all of us in a new reality because, by common consent, we agree that these specific words spoken in this particular context have the power to "make all things new."

A marriage is perhaps one of two instances in the modern world where we see the power of performative language. The other is seen in a courtroom. Picture the *Law and Order* scenario of the sentencing of a defendant. Before the jury returns its verdict, this person is presumed innocent and accorded the full weight of the law as a means to protect that presumed innocence. However, once the word *guilty* is pronounced over the very same person, many of the previously undeniable rights will disappear. Now the law that had been a bulwark of defense works to restrict and punish, and it is the spoken word which achieves this dramatic reversal of principles. And again, the power of the spoken word is found in the common consent of the people. It holds weight because we all agree that it does.

Previously, performative language operated in other venues of human existence. Greetings like "Good day" or "God be with you," function with the vestiges of the principle that the spoken word created the reality it described. Words once held great power. For example, when someone sneezes, why do we immediately tell them, "Bless you"? Surely it was because of the superstition that a sneeze expelled some of one's protective spirit. To shield the sneezer from the devil who might take advantage of a person thus less "inspirited" to enter into their soul, we say a benediction. The invocation of God's benediction had the power to thwart Satan.

The Lost Art of Performative Prayer

I imagine that many of us can both understand how performative language works and at the same time regret its diminishment in our world. It is a lost art that we vaguely recognize. Men tell each other that "a man's word is no longer his bond." Women tell each other that no one does what they say any longer.

I would add that the loss of performative language goes hand in hand with a dramatic shift that is currently taking place in the world of social ethics: the transformation of our society from a values-based community to one of compliance. Allow me to explain that by reference to a very familiar family story: in the fifteenth chapter of the Gospel of Luke there are three parables joined by a common set of themes. These three stories are given in explanation of Jesus' eating habits when authorities arrive with questions. In each we hear about something lost, something found, something celebrated. The first deals with a single sheep out of a herd of one hundred that goes missing. Then there is the loss of a single coin from a collection of ten. Finally, the chapter concludes with what might be the most familiar Christian parable: the story of the two sons.

"A certain man had two sons." That's how the parable begins. There is no title designating this as a story about a "prodigal" youngster. Jesus speaks to the conditions of the two sons and he is going to illustrate how both are lost. The younger of the two sons asks his father for his share of the family fortune prematurely. In that social matrix, the patriarch had to die before the division of assets could take place. This young kid is saying, "Dad. Drop dead," and meaning it quite literally.

Any self-respecting patriarch would have refused such a request without a second thought, as it was not only a personal affront, but also a serious breach of the publicly bestowed honor his family enjoys. Yet, this loving father grants the younger son's request and the boy goes off to spend his blood money. Now, he doesn't go to a righteous place like the temple in Jerusalem or holy sites in the desert. He heads off to the biblical equivalent of Las Vegas and wastes his inheritance on foolishness. When the money, food, and friends run out, he is lost, alone, and hungry.

Perhaps the most poignant word picture in the Christian corpus is the next phrase in this parable: "And coming to himself." Is that not a description of the maturing of the human heart? We come back to who we are and to whom we belong. We were never really lost for our home is always waiting in our heart, a heart made by God for the purpose of loving. The young man, now sober about his prospects and more aware of his previous actions, argues with himself that it is time to return to his father. He accepts that he has abrogated his place as a son, but he could contract himself with the father and become a worker in the fields. Surely his father would not turn him away. As a field hand there may not be much dignity but at least he won't starve to death. I picture the father, patron of an estate with many servants and slaves, like a fixture on a hilltop overlooking the road to distant lands. There he has been standing, year after year, hoping to see the returning silhouette of his youngest son on the horizon. And then one day, his dreams become a reality. The father is moved by deep compassion and runs out to embrace his returning boy.

It is perhaps difficult for our modern ears to understand the dramatic picture of a father racing down the road to his lost child. It would be like the chief partner in a Bay Street law firm walking out of his office on a cold January morning, wearing nothing but his underwear. Patriarchs in the time of Jesus presided over family disputes, they orchestrated high-level deals, presided over state dinners. They didn't go jogging and they certainly didn't display any overt affection for an ungrateful son who was obviously suffering his "just deserts." The first listeners to this story would have been surprised, affronted by the father's show of affection. In their minds, it was time for a little tough love. Make the kid grovel a bit. Make him eat a slice or two of humble pie.

Instead, the father seems bent upon celebration. The young man can barely get out the first line of the sentence of his confession before Dad takes over. He interrupts his boy in the line about offending heaven and calls the servants to bring out a robe to protect his shoulders. Can we get some rings to decorate his hands? Let's restore this kid's social position as the wealthy son of a loving father! Where are shoes for comforting his feet? How about killing the fatted calf? Let's party hearty.

And so, the tale of a lost son ends . . . or at least it could end at this stage. Indeed, as a perfect parallelism to the previous two parables in Luke 15, it ought to end when the lost is found. However, Jesus has more to say. There are two sons, after all. The first was lost to self-absorption and gratification. The second is also a piece of work, but in a different way.

Once the party begins, the older boy comes back to the house and hears the noise of a great celebration. Did you note that he doesn't go into the house to discover for himself what is happening? Nope, not this kid. He asks a servant, "What gives?" When he knows all the fuss is about his brother, he refuses to participate. Clearly, he is as lost as the younger son. But his prison is more complicated. He is not captive to self-indulgence. This boy's problem is self-righteousness—he knows he's right. Everything around him tells him so: the social principles of his household, the wisdom of his companions, and the spiritual dictums of his religion. They all remind him that he commands the high ground. And there is no question. He will not capitulate to his father's capricious abandonment of common sense. He will not join the party.

So, the head of the household has to swallow his pride a second time and go out again to greet his son. Apparently, the father performs his humiliation with grace, hardly reacting or missing a beat.

The older son has had some time to work himself into a lather of resentment. When the father entreats him to join the festivities, he blurts out in a disarmingly obvious show of filial envy. Can you imagine what it would have sounded like?

> Look here, old man! I have spent my days working for you like a slave. I have been your servant for all these years, doing my duty and what is my reward? I never get anything from you. I have been obedient to you and you never even gave me the means to have a small party amongst my friends. But when this *other* son of yours comes back—this son who wasted half of our land on booze, broads, and betting—what do you do? You throw him a blow-out party!

This single parable contains two of the most poignant lines in Scripture. The first we noticed was given to the son as "he comes to himself." The second is offered at this point. Instead of responding to his older son with frustration or sarcasm, the father again proves himself to be made entirely for loving. He says, "Son, everything I have is yours." Can there be any more profound statement of family loyalty and parental affection? What mother or father could put it more succinctly?

The parable ends here. We have no idea what the older son will do with his brother who was dead and is now alive, was lost and is found. Personally, my intuition tells me that the older brother stays out in the garden nursing his resentment. Alas, self-righteousness is one of the most difficult dungeons from which to make a jail break. It holds us tight and reminds us regularly that our intransigence is virtue. How many older brothers I have met: alone, angry, and absolutely convinced. How often do I see him in myself?

My point in recounting this parable is to recognize a common reaction of both brothers. Did you notice that in their interactions with their father they both seek to change the conditions of their relationship? When the young son rehearses his speech to himself he actually renounces his sonship, asks to be considered as servant. The older one calls himself a "slave." In each case, they are not living in the covenantal relationship with their father, but seek a contractual bond.

Imagine that the parable's meaning is hanging on this difference between covenantal and contractual relationships. Recall that it is told as a response to Jesus' table fellowship and his willingness to eat with anyone. His critics represent a very particular line of reasoning. Call it the sin/forgiveness trajectory. In this mode of thinking, there is a negotiated and respected spiritual exchange. To get God's forgiveness you have to perform certain acts of repentance and reflect specific attitudes of humility. The point of a contractual approach to spiritual wholeness is that we all follow prescribed rules. Believers exhibit modesty and obedience. In response God offers forgiveness and restitution. Of course, this need for humility and obsequiousness is orchestrated and evaluated by mediators. In the historical context of Jesus, it was the priests and scribes who acted as arbiters of God's acceptance. Your role as a devotee was to follow their instructions regarding one's sinfulness, and in return for your obedience to their "divinely inspired" regulations, you were blessed with absolution. A deal made on earth and sanctified by heaven.

The two sons are living by this understanding of forgiveness and sin. They impute this understanding to the father as would most members of the audience who first heard this parable. It's all about making and sustaining a contractual relationship.

Jesus and his kingdom movement are moving along another pathway. Call it the human creature lost human creature now found trajectory. In this case, God is not concerned about deals over forgiveness. No contracts. This deity does not wait in heaven for human beings to perform a specific ritual or emotional gymnastics. The God of the Covenant is focused entirely on those who are lost and how to help them find their way home.

If a covenantal approach to human relationships sounds extravagant, imagine yourself with a teenager who has gone missing, either lost geographically or emotionally. Will you spend your time listing the many rituals, rules, and regulations you will impose upon them once they come back? Do you go on television and tell this lost child that you'll gladly receive them home as long as they straighten up? Of course not. Your entire energy is focused on finding them, holding them, and never letting them go so far away again. You want them to know how important they are. How much they are loved. Contracts be damned! We just want our lost children to come home.

If we can feel the strong pull of a covenantal relationship, how much more the Creator of all?

The parable is foundational to the kingdom of God movement because it underlines the basis for this new relationship of human beings. We are bound by love and common purpose. Once we resort to contractual agreements we have lost the essential qualities of trust and passion, qualities that characterize all lasting human endeavors.

The Decline in the Power of Words

Now the current decline in performative language is surely connected to a shift in self-understanding. Our modern world has drifted away from covenantal language and practice to contractual ones. There was once a time when words had power to bind people together in a community because our words were spoken within covenantal relationship and assumed the stabilizing and formative emotional connections of faith and trust that characterized that relationship. "Our word was our bond," and certain shared words reminded us that we were bound by common purpose. Values need not, therefore, be overtly described nor prescribed by written contract.

When the mind-set of the older brother dominates our society, we shift away from the covenantal thinking of the father, imposing what is called "compliance" reasoning. This approach assumes that the only way to ensure virtue among individuals is to document it: create a list of acceptable behaviors, agree on these principles, sign our names, and live by the principles we have enumerated. At this point our spoken words have no power unless they find some final formula in a written document. Even then, our contracts have little moral agency. They are simply rules to direct behavior, lacking the capacity to invent, create, or establish new conventions and covenants.

It is the dominance of compliance thinking that has blunted our ability as Christians to see language as a means for human transformation. When we gather in church, our spoken words are a recital of well-established ideas—but no one expects them to change us in any real way. And so, as I mentioned above, the Prayer is more like a mind-numbing mantra than an agent of change.

The Prayer as Performative Language

I want you to go back with me to the first century, to a "kingdom Movement" gathering. You'll find no find Christians here, no distinct church. Not yet. If you're looking for a religion on which to peg your perceptions, you might detect vague overtones of a Jewish synagogue in this circle. These people call themselves "the Way."[1] They're meeting in a small shop that also serves as a home for a leather merchant. Its main door faces a commercial street and its back wall is attached to a larger family compound.

These "kingdom" groups meet regularly. Some gather every night, others have settled on a special evening once a week.

It's dark. The work day is done and we're hurrying along the street to make it to "the Way" in time for the shared meal, a potluck consisting of all the food that we have. That's how this religious group operates. No stinting, no dragging out the leftovers from last night's festivities. Everything! Mind you, given the lack of refrigeration and food preservatives, "all that we have" can easily be carried in our arms or, if we're very fortunate, a basket or two.

We run because, aside from wanting to avoid tardiness, we don't want to miss a single moment. Since we have joined this group, our lives have been transformed. We are no longer afraid of the Romans—or the Herodians[2] for that matter. Our kids don't go hungry anymore, and we have discovered a spiritual freedom that has the power to heal the broken, blamed, and shamed. Each time we gather, we have no idea what might happen; anything is possible.

We greet one another with warm hugs and kisses and then we set out the food. Before we share our meal, we pray this special prayer Jesus gave us.

We go slowly through the words, but when it comes to the phrase "Thy kingdom come" there is the briefest of pauses. This is the reverent moment when we call ourselves into being. We're not wishing for a future event; this is not a petition for a distant event or potential hope. This is a statement of our reality. Like the phrase used in common meals, "Let us eat," the phrase "Thy kingdom come" is a statement of fact. It is present tense. The community is reconstituting itself.

Imagine, if you would, a gathering of people who, "by common consent," agree to be God's kingdom on earth. Not as a theory, not as a great idea, but as a *socially binding* and spiritually transformative community. They are no longer Judeans in Roman-occupied Galilee, they are citizens of

1. This is the name given to the kingdom of God movement described by the author of Acts (Acts 24:14).

2. It is difficult to know about this group exactly. Certainly, they represented a conservative, monarchial, political party. More than likely they were the collaborators who preserved Herod's attitude toward the occupying forces: collaboration for political self-preservation and economic advancement.

God's land. They follow God's reign and live their lives in accordance with the trust, loyalty, and reverence that God the King requires.

Of course, like other circumstances mentioned above, a marriage or court, if we were to study the minute physiological or neurological details of each person present in the kingdom gathering we would realize that nothing had changed. However, the common purpose and joint consent of the group have made all the difference. There is no way to avoid the simple fact that the people are now changed. They have arrived at and are living in a new promised land.

Recite "Thy kingdom come!" and . . . it does! Quite literally.

Come back with me to the twenty-first century for a moment. Do you need a glass of water? How about a little bit of bread? Somehow, we should stop ourselves in midstream right here and give this notion our full attention. Performative language requires a good think. Why not pause at this point? Lay this book down and go for a long walk, hold the hand of a loved one, watch the river, the fire, the mountains—do whatever helps you to reflect on important principles!

Imagine what it would be like to join a community that literally reconstitutes itself as the company of God's citizens. How would that feel? What would we do differently?

In the next few chapters, we turn to the Prayer again to fill in the details of how "thy kingdom come" is actually made concrete and operational.

As a final tidbit of information on which to reflect before we close, let us recognize that performative language works on two levels: personal and corporate. I suspect that the current malaise of historic churches in North America is actually functioning on both these same planes as well.

Personally, we don't actually *believe* our own words. We expect *not* to be changed by them. While we publicly claim that our whole purpose is to have these words turn us into a "new community," we personally hope that they won't. Corporately, we do not hold ourselves accountable for the cohesiveness and extent of the "kingdom" community we profess to want God to send us. Church is a collection of individual tastes and talents. It is not a common cause and is even less a communal life.

Our lack of belief in the power of ours words arises from familiarity. As with my jokes, the stories have become so familiar to us that we are no longer moved. We turn to that problem next.

5

Relationships: "Our Father"

No Surprises . . . Yet

ONE OF THE LONG-TERM handicaps of any religious tradition is that, over time, it tends to reduce the mystery of its truth. I am sure this is not intentional. Quite the contrary! Religions survive on the creation and re-creation of wonder in their devotees, but there is no getting around memory. As believers accumulate traditions and rituals, they quite naturally tame the wilder sides of the "Awe-filling Presence" they worship. This being the case, it is accurate to suggest that as Christians we have trouble hearing our story because it no longer surprises us. We know the punch line of all our jokes, so to speak, having told and retold them to ourselves and our grandchildren for centuries.

In a similar fashion, we have a serious hurdle to overcome in our understanding of Scripture in general—the Prayer in particular. Since we think we know what the good book contains and what the famous prayer actually means, we are in danger of putting the em-*pha*-sis on the wrong syl-*la*-ble.

For this reason, I believe that when we read the Scripture, one of the chief impediments to understanding is our faith itself. It's not atheism or antagonism, it is our faith that gets in the way of appreciating how radical the good news can be. Modern Christians are the inheritors of over 2,000 years of tradition and centuries of theological interpretation that tell us what we should think. Opening the Bible, we already know what we will find in its pages. As believers, we have been taught to see the Scriptures as testimony to or evidence of the power and glory of God made manifest in Jesus Christ. We've been taught that the Gospels hit their high point in the message that Jesus was crucified for our sins. In three days, he rose from the dead, living in all eternity as our judge and our hope. He is the salvation of our souls and waits for us in heaven along with our loved ones. We read the Psalms and the prophets—even the Torah as foreshadowing of that Good Friday/Easter event. So, we open the Bible expecting to find Jesus, no matter which chapter and/or verse we fall upon.

There once was a minister who was intimidated by the obligatory "children's time" in the service. The kids had him absolutely unnerved, the fact that all of his stories were thinly veiled versions of the same Sunday school moralism—"Jesus loves me; this I know, for the Bible tells me so"—notwithstanding.

One Sunday was particularly bad. He began by asking the circle of children what was "brown and furry, hopped across your front lawn, had a long bushy tail and chewed nuts?" One bright boy in the second row shot his hand up and waved it excitedly. The minister, seeing an eager soul wanting to embrace his Saviour, said, "Okay, Johnny! What's brown and furry, hops across your front lawn, has a long bushy tail and chews nuts?"

"Well," replied Johnny, "It sounds a lot like a squirrel, but I'll bet it's Jesus."

In our more simplistic expressions, that is how Christianity has taught its followers to read the Bible: it's all about Jesus, our Savior, and his salvation of my soul.

If we *think* we know what is happening, and when we are assured that the final purpose of Holy Scripture will be Jesus, we are in danger of misinterpretation. If every chapter and verse in the Bible is pointing to the Easter event, then we could undermine our ability to hear the surprises implanted in the story by the Gospel writers. If every parable has to end in Jesus no matter where it has begun, our intellectual convictions will suffer from serious simplification. Such shallow thinking is not just tragic; it can also result in dangerously misguided action. Under the influence of this monocular reading of Scripture we can easily fall into supersessionism[1] and religious intolerance.

---

1. Supersessionism is the Christian practice of seeing Judaism as nothing more than the first expression of God's will and covenant and that the Christian covenant in Jesus supersedes the Jewish one—hence discounting Judaism as a past and "rejected" religious expression of faith.

Of course, what we have done to Scripture can also happen to our understanding of God. For entire lifetimes, we have taken our relationship with God for granted. After years of familiarity with the Maker of the Universe we can take certain terms and approaches for granted. God is my "Father!" What else is new? God "forgives me my debts." Of course, what else would God do? Familiarity breeds contempt or at least disregard and so we have house trained our God into domesticity.

Let's pause before we begin a verse-by-verse examination of the Prayer and recognize that what Jesus proposes as a prayer has two astounding principles which we all but ignore.

First, the Prayer says absolutely nothing about Jesus, his power to save us, or our need to embrace him as "Lord." There is no narrative detail about Jesus or reference to his disciples. The entire purpose of the Prayer seems to focus away from anything we might recognize as "Christian." In fact, this is a very Jewish prayer. We are speaking to the God of the Torah, and one could easily pray this prayer in a synagogue without serious offense. We address God as an intimate relationship, not a hypothetical principle. The Prayer praises this God's majesty and rule over both the heavens and the earth (Ps 121). It touches on economic principles drawn from Leviticus and Deuteronomy. There are overtones of the twenty-third psalm and reminders of the chosen people's journey through the wilderness into the promise and liberation of a new land.

If we can peel back two millennia of "Christian" ritual recitations, the original prayer shines like a succinct statement of Jewish trust and devotion.

The second remarkable fact of the Prayer is that it introduces an astoundingly refreshing relationship with the Maker of the Universe. We take the initial introductory phrase of the Prayer for granted. "Our Father who art in heaven." Imagine if I were to suggest that it was now possible, indeed desirable, to write a personal note to the Queen of England. No more diplomatic red tape. No protocol officers or regal receptions. Don't wait in line or line the streets as she passes by in a bulletproof limousine. Just send her an e-mail directly! "Hey Lizzie . . . what's up?"

Then add to this stunning effrontery the unquestioning assumption that the queen would both appreciate our directness and make immediate response. Is it possible to start an e-mail correspondence with the queen? Why not begin a "royal chat" on Facebook? I wonder if she would follow me on Twitter or appreciate being part of my Instagram circle?

If you're squirming with embarrassment or shaking your head with disbelief, you have some measure of the innovation of the Prayer. It breaks through centuries of religious practice. We are going straight to the top of Mount Sinai to repeat Moses's feat of speaking face-to-face with our Maker. Can you imagine how breathtaking the Prayer can be? It breaks down hitherto unrelenting barriers[2] and opens up a new world to the believer.

We will speak of the theological importance of the innovation of the Prayer in a few moments. My point at this stage in our work is simply to hold out the importance of *surprise*. If our religious practice has suffered from an anemic belief in itself and its own story, this sickness has been further deteriorated by our domestication of surprise.

Of course, the loss of surprise is not the fault of churchgoers or theologians—we are all victims of history. However, it is *our* problem and the reason for this text. How do we reinvest the excitement of the impossible possibility in our personal devotion and public witness?

While I write these words, I have just come from a protestant Cuban worship service. Held in the charming community of Luyanó Reformed Presbyterian Church, from all outward signs, it could have been a liturgy devised and conducted in North America. Apart from the fact that it is all in Spanish, the liturgical order, succession of prayers, and even some of the hymn melodies reflect a very sober, rational approach to worship. John Calvin would be right at home here. We sang the Lord's Prayer to a modern tune,[3] which was a clever innovation, but it was again very Western in flavor. There could be little question that this denomination and local congregation had inherited a great deal of its material from missionary founders, all of whom came from the United States. They brought their piety and practice down to this beautiful island, translated it into Spanish, and away they went!

But when we left the well-worn path of English American Protestantism, suddenly a new spirit arose. You could see it, feel it, and hear it. We stopped singing "This is my Father's World" and began a very Cuban tune: "Si Vale la Pena de Vivir" ("Yes, it's Worth the Pain to Live"). Suddenly, the place broke into a rhythm and volume that's nothing but salsa. Cymbals which had previously been kept under the pews were brought out.

2. One must be cautious here. The approach of Jesus is innovative, even radical—but it is not original. It is entirely Jewish. The Torah and even more so the Psalms are filled with examples of intimacy between Creator and creaturely salutations.

3. They use the tune "The House of the Rising Sun," and set it to an adapted translation of the Lord's Prayer that is found in the appendix.

People stopped reading the text and started clapping their hands. Bodies began to sway and move in the delightfully sensual way that only Cubans can achieve. Now the Spirit was alive. I am not suggesting that the North American heritage of the Presbyterian Cuban Reformed church is wrong or misguided. It is obviously a treasured inheritance, but it lacks the life and vibrancy of their indigenous spirit of joy and dance. It is this surprisingly animated Presence that is missing from traditional Christian expressions in North America. All too often there is no "lift" or genuine delight in our practice. A well-executed performance or an ornately eloquent expression of devotion cannot substitute for the simple breathtaking surprise of creativity. The spontaneous Spirit trumps reason every time.

So, let us begin our line-by-line examination of the Prayer, looking and hoping to find a surprise in every line.

A God of Community

The opening invocation is, at first glance, entirely predictable and unassuming. "Our Father who art in heaven"—nothing new here. We know the words by heart and one has only to recite that first phrase and everyone will join in automatically.

"Our" Father is first-person plural. God is a God of the community. For the initial community of disciples, it would have been quite inconceivable to start with a first-person singular address. God may be singular, but the human creature cannot be understood in his or her singularity. The first surprise is slow to take hold or even recognize. Our Creator is in *dialogue*, not monologuing—a "group chat," so to speak. We come to this God as part of a group.

Again, this is very Jewish. The history of Israel is the story of a people, enslaved in Egypt, lost in the wilderness, exiled in Babylon; the community grew according to its corporate identity as God's chosen ones—not a group of individuals, but a *community* of faith.

There are several dimensions to this collective personality. In ancient times, the people are their leader and their leader, in a particular fashion, represents the people. The health of the king was everyone's concern, for in the king's well-being rested the well-being of the whole nation. In this sense, the indiscretion of King David became the people's sin. It is possible to read the history of God's chosen ones as the rise and fall of a king's morality. With David, we reach the pinnacle of God's favor, and then, once he takes Bathsheba and she gives birth to Solomon, the fortunes of the people slide, falling from one dilemma into another until they suffer the indignity of successive occupations by marauding empires.

All of the people suffer the nation's humiliation. They do not disassociate themselves from the collective, blaming leaders and divorcing themselves from the misfortunes of the nation as a whole.

In a similar fashion, the effrontery of the younger son in the parable of the two sons (Luke 15) is spread over the entire family. Everyone suffers his shame, and all hope that the father will put him in his place because, in this manner, *everyone* is restored to honor and health. In this light, the father's extravagant love is costly, not just for him personally, but for the entire clan. He welcomes them, probably unwillingly, into a new way of being family.

A second consequence of a corporate personality is that you begin your self-understanding with a focus that is decidedly farsighted. Your eyes look to the horizon of the people. It's a natural reaction for the first-century community of disciples. It's not that individuals did not experience personal doubts and delights, but these feelings were subsumed under an entirely different structure of self-understanding.

I find myself stretching to get my mind around this idea. Why don't we sit down to breakfast and think about it? At my early morning kitchen table, there is a teenager. He's got a heart of gold and such a tender sense of emotional well-being. I can't fault him, but at this stage in his life and at this point in the day he is absolutely and entirely self-absorbed. There is no world outside his own needs, desires, and anxieties. Looking into his eyes, I can see nothing more than a self-directed worldview. It's not that he's exceptionally egotistical. He's a teenager—it comes with the territory.

Have you been there? Those of us who have raised children know about teenage self-absorption and the annoying thing about self-absorption is that it *is* so self-absorbed! Ask my boy about the night before and you get a monosyllabic response. How about school? Same thing. Try to start a debate about world events, racial justice, family responsibilities—it all gets funneled through the narrow perspective of his personal concerns. If it isn't in his world, it isn't. There can be no other starting place. Ask him about performing a household chore and it's all about how he is "so busy" and tired. Argue that we should reach out to a neighbor in need and he asks why he has to do that *right now*. Point out that the world is coming to an end and he will ask if that means he doesn't have to brush his teeth today. Early mornings are all about satiating personal needs.

Keep in mind this unrelenting singularly of a teenage perspective (and please hear that I also know how deeply and sincerely young people feel about people and circumstances outside their close circle). In its unquestioning and insistent focus, it is an example of how human beings are shaped by our basic worldview and frame of reference.

In first-century Palestine, we have to reverse the perspective 180 degrees and keep the same persistent resolve. The impossibility of thinking about self first. Whatever happens in the day—taxes, the search for work, cooking, or cleaning—it is all a reflection of the corporate self and soul. Indeed, this reflects another obstacle to understanding the matrix of the world within which Jesus helped the lost and healed the broken. No one in that society was thinking about getting ahead with an individual ambition or hoarding their personal fortune. Of course, you could do those things and some people did, but these were the unfortunate exceptions. Almost everyone else was working within the collective. If you desired wealth, it was for the purpose of restoring or consolidating family fortunes. Honor was a group sport.

We mouth the initial words of the Prayer and the modern mind mostly has no clue how to return to the place where the "our" of our lives extends beyond the nuclear family and a small circle of friends. This is perhaps the second obstacle to hearing the gospel. First, we are too well-fed to taste the radical and refreshing nature of Jesus' good news about the bread of life. And now, we face the issue of *social cohesion*. It's too loose in the North American standard of living. We'd like more solidarity, but we have lost the tools to achieve it.

Are you still sitting at the table with my son? Let's leave that first-world kitchen and head down south. We're going to encounter the vestiges of the corporate personality in a third-world context. It also happens in the kitchen. Cuba has been my "home" for a decade or more, and in that country, there are many problems: overcrowding, bureaucratic inefficiency, economic duplicity. I know many of the problems, sometimes firsthand. Nevertheless, there is something incredibly beautiful and reassuring in the extent to which necessity has created an unquestioning assumption of human solidarity.

For example: In North America, grandparents are largely an obligation for grandchildren. We go visit when we are asked, however frequent or infrequent that may be. We put on a brave face and a false smile, and trade polite diminutives: "Oh, isn't that nice!" Can you hear the duplicity and boredom that are standard practice in "the visit to Gramma's house"? It is an obligation and we are more or less happy to do it and just as happy for it to be over. But in Cuba, grandparents are a treasure. You call them daily and visit them often. Their aches and pains are yours to bear and relieve. I have watched as a granddaughter gave all of her early morning free time in order to fix a grandmother's breakfast. Grown men have cried in my office because they could not see their grandfather often enough. The relationship is not colored by duty. It is one that is shaped by true devotion. Grandparents play a role which is much closer to that of a parent.

In a similar fashion, one's compassion for family members expands to include a circle of friends so that the demands of one individual's circumstances are embraced and carried by all. A cousin's boyfriend has a claim on your time and loyalty. His motorbike breaks and he needs a lift to work—you offer it without regret or recrimination. A neighbor's husband leaves and the woman's kids need care for a few hours each day while she works. It happens. Someone comes up with some free time, or a grandmother offers to take them in. The child-rearing is shared or bartered for other services. Once you are welcomed in, you are carried with the expectation that you will take up your share of the common burden of "making" this life a living.

There's an Internet chain letter doing the rounds that has captured this distinctive spirit. It's a generalized comparison about friends and one line is: A Canadian friend knocks on the door to be let in, but a Cuban friend opens the door and shouts out, "I'm here." A Canadian friend asks if you can make coffee. But a Cuban friend goes into the kitchen, puts on the coffee pot, and then asks a neighbor for some sugar to go with.

Over the past few years, I have been part of an ongoing interchange between Cubans and Canadians, and I have watched this social solidarity grow. It is infectious. Most northerners long for that sense of security, to be part of a social group larger than the four walls in which they live—a circle of family and friends that actually means business. You see, we are all so completely self-contained. We don't need a larger community even though we desperately long for it. And our Cuban ambassadors have taught us how to build on our dreams of social solidarity and actually live it.

I recall how a single mother in my circle was faced with juggling shift work and child care. It seemed impossible. Every week, her resources were being depleted and the Cuban in our midst said, "We'll all help out." The mother replied that she had no money to pay for help and the Cuban replied that "taking care of kids is not about money, for heaven's sake!" The message was clear: "You are never alone!"

Sure, such a "crowded" life comes with drawbacks. Privacy is a rare commodity. Gossip is as common as the air you breathe. Yes, in Cuba this social solidarity is a function of economic necessities and the housing crisis of a third-world community; nevertheless it is equally true that you are never alone. Never.

Therefore, we remind ourselves that the Prayer begins with the affirmation that we are never alone. It is not "my" God who is heaven, but "our" Father. And in the light of the performative language that shapes this prayer, it is not a stretch to say that its first words establish a community. Not wishful thinking of a paradise "somewhere over the rainbow." The Prayer begins with a "we" that is immediately practical and delightfully rich.

A God in Heaven?

Perhaps here we need to add a footnote about the Prayer's realm of influence. It is a here-and-now exercise. Our God may be "in heaven," but apparently, the focus of the Prayer is down here on earth. We say much more about this in the next chapter. At this point, let us avoid any confusion because of this initial invocation. Our father "in heaven" is simply a way to designate which parent is being addressed.

Let there be no doubt. We are not participating in a covert form of ancestor worship. Jesus is not calling out to Joseph. We are not addressing earthly parents.

Rather than being biological or adoptive, this Father is "in heaven."

The one who is being addressed is the God who is both Creator of heaven and earth and the Lord of Life. No question. We're on a direct line to our Maker.

Okay, we have the theory of corporate personality and performative language, but there is something missing: practice.

A God Found in Community

One of my favorite classes focuses on kissing. When I teach engineers about ethics we arrive at a very important learning: the difference between theory and practice. I ask them to write a five-step manual to kissing. They see this as an eminently reasonable exercise, since every human action is benefited by clear instructions.

The lecture begins with all kinds of statistics about kissing. Did you know that in a single kiss there is an exchange of 264 colonies of bacteria? That the longest kiss lasted over twenty-nine hours? How about this? The term "French" kiss came from the early twentieth century when Puritans on this side of the ocean assumed that the French were oversexed and therefore anything beyond a respectful peck on the lips was too sensual to be considered American.

But have you ever tried to describe how you kiss? What are the actual steps? Do you teach you kids? How many of us pull out a parental self-help book and read to our children about the steps for achieving the perfect kiss? We spend endless hours poring over expert advice on everything from toilet training to piano lessons. Why not kissing?

So, I set my engineers the task of writing just such a manual. Give me five succinct steps. Something we can put with our driver's license: a handy pocket-sized guide. So, when the occasion arises, we can review the essential steps to kissing before engaging in any serious application of the theory.

They usually come up with some variation of the following incredibly sterile list:

The kiss-er approaches the kiss-ee and achieves a geographic proximity that allows for appropriate physical contact between each participant's lips, while also establishing the possibility of ancillary appropriate sensual stimulation.

Establish stable structural stability between kiss-er and kiss-ee such that when the kissing action begins neither party will be overbalanced or uncomfortable. This structural stability can be achieved through intertwined hands, mutual lateral support of arms placed firmly on reciprocal shoulders or backs.

Achieve permission for the procedure to continue either through nonverbal eye contact or intentional invitational phrases such as: "May I kiss you now?" "Would you like to kiss?" "How about a goodnight kiss?" Be careful not to rush this initial invocation of interest, especially when relying on nonverbal clues.

Pursing lips, the kiss-er leans in closer to the kiss-ee. Do not rush. Allow the physiological chemistry to build toward higher levels of emotional agitation. It is suggested that the kiss-er begin to close eyes once kiss-ee's lips are within range.

Final contact. In this final stage, the kiss-er's lips establish contact with the kiss-ee's lips. Eyes are now completely closed. It is suggested that the lateral supports increase in pressure to pull bodies into close structure contact. Such mutual stability is necessary since it is often the case the contact of the kiss-er's lips upon those of the kiss-ee excites neurological stimulants which give one a momentary light-headedness.

In my lecture, I read out this list with utter seriousness and then I ask the obvious question. Now that I have described the theory and process of kissing, you all know all about it, right?

There's general laughter, and then someone in the back row, who has appeared to be sleeping, but who is actually very bright, will shout back:

"No. You don't know anything about kissing until you've been kissed."

That is the distinction I was looking to underline. The theory of something so intimate as kissing can never compare to the practice. The event is everything. We might choose to describe it afterwards, and there is some satisfaction in that exercise, but let no one be fooled. The exchange of theoretical information is worthless when compared to the actual participation in the moment.

And this is the truth of Jesus' invitation to pray to God like a Father. Set aside the gender and exact relationship for the moment and focus on the idea of addressing God as a being, not a theoretical substance. Substantive thinking establishes categories and attributes for God. It describes God with elaborate adjectival phrases. In such a way, we achieve intellectual rigor and accuracy.

I have heard prayers that begin by addressing the Almighty as "the source of all life." This is a very accurate description; a bit of exceptionally clear theory. But no one prays *to a theory*. Likewise, language such as: "Ground of Being," "the Mystery beyond all Understanding" or "Creator of all that Is," are all clear and true statements of theology but have no ability to actually relate God's essence.

Take people 10,000 feet above the ground in an airplane and throw them out into the air, and I guarantee, no one will shout out, "Oh Spirit of Unknowing."

The issue is simple. God is not a noun. God is a *verb*.

Christian theology is essentially relational. All that we say about God or Christ, the church, the end of history, or human salvation, it all boils down to relational concepts. We are exploring a living Being, not a scientific formula, and therefore all our concepts will have that coloring. In our anguish, we call out to God who is like a mother or father, friend, sister or brother.

The hope, indeed the real expectation of the Prayer, is to establish and enhance the relationship between the believer and their God.

A note of caution is required here. At this stage, there will be some who would agree with the principle of Christian theology being essentially all about relationships. They invite themselves and others into a "personal" relationship with Jesus in which their personal desires and ambitions are lost with the joy and mystery of a "closer walk with thee." Any examination of this relationship created by faith is construed as a lack of trust or an intellectualization. Don't ask, just be!

However true this may feel, the actual evidence points in another direction: relationships are deepened by reason, not diminished by it. Our faith in another being is always seeking to understand itself. All our hopes and dreams, while largely unspoken and beyond the realm of cognition, nevertheless need to be expressed and shared. That's how love grows.

The same can be true for the relationship created with "Our Father." The experience of communion with God is central, but it becomes either nostalgic sentimentalism or self-serving emoting if there is no intentional attempt to examine its relative merits. It's not a lack of faith that motivates this exploration, but quite the opposite. The more we believe, the more we want to know *how* and *why* and *when* we believe. The introduction of serious questioning strengthens any relationship, including and especially the one we have with our Father.

But let us be clear. The challenge in liberal Protestant circles is usually not the acceptance of a theoretical approach to belief. Our problem is the belief itself. We are on unstable ground when it comes to relying on and living in the relationship with God. For this reason, I would emphasize again the centrality of performative language. The Prayer is not a clever bit of Christian theology—a spiritual creed in "four easy verses." This is an encounter, not an idea. Personally, the hardest part of my spiritual journey is always to allow the encounter to overtake me and let the relationship grow and deepen without the interference of substantive reasoning.

Perhaps our greater experience with the theoretical side of praying has made us sensitive to a final dimension we must address in this first invocative phrase: gendered vocabulary.

Metaphorical Language

In recent years, we have become advisedly aware of the damaging, sometimes punitive, power of "gendered" language. When we pray to a "Father," there are some in the community for whom this is not a positive relationship. Alas, there have been far too many fathers or father figures who have abused their position. Young men and women have been victims of abuse, both physical and emotional. In the worst instances, addressing God as Father can be like being re-victimized. In less stressful cases, God portrayed as a male is an unhelpful reminder of a troubled relationship. Either way, the use of masculine imagery to describe our God as a "Father" can make praying impossible for some.

So, to achieve an inclusive worshipping community where all are safe, it is necessary to add female imagery to address our Maker. Some people argue that we undermine the historicity of the Prayer when we change the ancient words. They claim we are acting out of a faddish impulse. While I have sympathy for tradition and the need to hallow it, the principle of justice, including all and welcoming all, trumps any historical sensitivity. Besides, the Prayer is not an unassailable, sacred icon. It is a dynamic event that, by necessity, must grow with the exigencies of the community

Others claim that inclusive language is often clumsy and shallow. It lacks the depth of spiritual reverence that only comes from long practice and the refinement of years of worship. To these objections, I would reply that eventually we will gain a new level of linguistic beauty even while using inclusive language. I am ready to put up with current awkwardness for the sake of a long-term correction in our liturgical practice.

Other people find the use of male images is an unfortunate restriction of the nature of God. While the Bible is decidedly patriarchal, it is not exclusively so. There are many possible female images, often metaphors, which are used to describe the nature of God: God is like a mother hen protecting her chicks (Isa 31:5, Matt 23:37), or feminine figure of wisdom (Job 28). Sometimes God is portrayed as a female lover (Song 4:1). Given the potential for greater depth in biblical images which portray God as both male and female, surely it is near-sighted and narrow-minded to focus simply on God as a "Father."

I find the variety of images for God in current use to be both refreshing and necessary for spiritual growth. There are only a few precautions. First, it is unfortunate if, in our search for inclusive images, we undermine the foundational relational nature of our encounter with God. I can pray to

God who is a "song of beauty" or a "lover of every soul" or a "handmaid of peace." Eloquence notwithstanding, when I am desperate I would never call out for "my song of beauty." It's a "Dad" or "Mom" that I need. In a similar fashion calling God our "friend" or "guide" undercuts the intimacy and loyalty that are clearly the key features of a God who is our parent. Whatever we do, our language needs to somehow capture both the immediacy and trust of a child/parent relationship.

Given the many questions and doubts about exclusive language in the Prayer, it becomes difficult to know how to be faithful to the ancient tradition and yet honor the need for inclusive language. There is no easy solution apart from abandoning the Prayer all together. I have adopted a partial solution in dropping the word "Lord" from my description of this prayer. Jesus, by the way, gives it no title. "The Lord's Prayer" is a Christian church designation. For some time, I chose to pray to Our Father/Mother God who art in heaven. It was clumsy but the best I could devise. A student solved the problem with a theological corrective. She pointed out that all images for God are metaphorical. No one has seen God (except Moses, perhaps), and so all of the language we use has to describe a Being that is beyond our comprehension. Any adjective, noun, or verb will fall short of capturing the nature of God. Even while we have enjoyed the security of a tradition of praying to "Our Father," we need to be reminded that even this image, given to us by Christ, is also metaphorical. Surely Jesus knew very well that God is "like" a father, but God is also so much more than this image can portray. So, my student suggested we introduce the Prayer by explaining the metaphorical nature of God language. She said that "we pray to God who is like our Father." I added a little bit of an introduction, and the final result goes something like this: "We pray to God who is like our Mother, gathering her children close, and we pray to God who is like our Father who art in heaven . . . ." A compromise surely, but one that retains the relational nature of our encounter with God and yet balances out our language.

One final note. I have sometimes been invited to pray to "Dad." Jesus uses a very familiar Aramaic term *Abba* with respect to his parent in heaven. When he prays in the garden while his disciples are sleeping, it is to his *Abba* or "Dad." I find this quite comforting and would have no objection to inserting this diminutive into the Prayer. "Our Dad who is heaven" does reflect the surprise that must have gripped the initial audience who asked Jesus about praying.

There are more surprises to come, many which have been lost to modern ears. The centuries of repetition have numbed us to the very obvious direction of the petitions which follow the introductory salutations. The next line of the Prayer is a case in point: "Thy will be done on earth as it is in heaven." Let us now turn to that verse and see how our theology has muddied the waters of this clear proposition.

6

A Materialist Religion:
"Thy will be done on earth . . ."

A Pastor's Story

YOUNG FRANK'S FUNERAL WAS the worst I have ever attended. He was taken too soon, at eighteen years old.

What a waste. Frank was far too promising for anyone to resort to the well-worn condolences about God taking someone in their proper time. His life was stolen! His dreams and ambitions—all yet to be fulfilled: a beautiful girlfriend, a large scholarship to study abroad. Everything! What could be said that would make sense out of the sheer horror of his death? At such tragic times, it is best to say nothing or as little as possible. Any theological argument about God's endless promises would be pointless. Exhortation to carry on in the face of personal hardship would be hollow and meaningless. Stunned silence would have been best. But human beings, like nature itself, abhor a vacuum. And so, we filled the void in our hearts with words, too many words.

Picture a summer night. No moon to cast light on the road. Frank and his girlfriend were coming back into town to celebrate his grandparents' anniversary. What a loyal kid—selfless even though he hadn't passed twenty. On a lonely stretch of four-lane highway, where there should never have been a problem, he hit a moose. Colliding head-on with the beast, it rolled the car, killing Frank instantly and sending his girlfriend into the intensive care ward of the local hospital.

We waited a week for the funeral. Relatives from a great distance had to gather. It's not uncommon when a teenager dies. No one was expecting this horror. Siblings and cousins were scattered across the country at summer jobs. Travel times and tickets had to be arranged, and so we waited. Fortunately, Frank's girlfriend recovered quickly. She would have many months of rehabilitation, but apart from the emotional damage, she was expected to recover "fully." My part in the funeral was simply to comfort the grandparents who were close friends. The funeral itself would be performed by a colleague.

Half an hour before the service began, the sanctuary was full. More seats were brought in to accommodate people along the front and back. We filled the choir loft. I could see at least one high-ranking politician. The story of Frank's death had captured the imagination of the city and so it was a funeral not to be missed. Plates of sandwiches waited in the parlor. Latecomers began to spill out into the vestibule. Everything was hushed.

If only it had stayed that way.

The funeral began with the traditional entry of the closest family members. In came Frank's parents. Then the two grandparents appeared, followed by Frank's siblings and uncles and aunts. Lastly, a few cousins. Then there was a commotion at the door and in came his girlfriend. The congregation, who had just sat down, stood again as if with one mind—we wanted to show our respect to her. Frank's girlfriend needed the help of a couple of friends. The one on the left was pushing an IV pole while supporting her with an arm around her shoulder. On the right, a friend carried an extra pillow with her free hand. Frank's girlfriend winced her way across the front of the church into a place of honor. As she shuffled along we could all feel her pain. I believe if we had ended the funeral right there with our reverent silence, it would have been perfect.

However, you can never leave a perfect thing alone and so the minister began the worship service. We went through the predictable Bible passages, a subdued solo from a family friend, and a very delicate and touching homily about God's pain in the world.

Then all hell broke loose. The minister decided—on his own or at the behest of the family, I never discovered the culprit—to open up the floor and invite anyone who wanted to speak to come forward. I imagine the desire was to allow people a chance to voice their sorrow. Good intentions. We know where *that* pathway leads.

The first was an aunt who began by saying that she didn't know whether she should tell her story or not. That is always a warning sign. If you have to begin with that kind of introduction the answer is always, "No!" Frank's aunt served up fifteen minutes of inside family jokes and incongruous expressions of regret. Then a cousin stood up and offered a poem. I would like to be generous, but it was a bit of sentimental drivel. Next a scout leader. He pulled out a long list of badges won by the deceased. Frank would have been proud. His girlfriend hobbled up and cried for five minutes. And that opened the flood gates. The line-up at the microphone grew longer with each new speaker.

I suppose I was ready to listen to close relations who wanted or needed to grieve publicly—especially the girlfriend. It's tough, but understandable. However, I draw the line at off-the-cuff-theology: cheap answers to life's very costly questions. We were subjected to countless heresies in the one hour and twenty minutes that ensued. Three Neoplatonists insisted Frank's body was now gone, but his spirit was alive with God in heaven. A Stoic argued that the spark of his soul was still with us. Nice! A couple of Ebionite Christians insisted that Frank was a gift while he was alive and that's all we can expect. We ended with a Docetist who said Frank was never actually "with" us because his "real" place was with his Father in heaven.

Awful theology! None of it particularly helpful or Christian.

When that funeral blessedly came to a close, I realized that there was a great need to state again the principles behind the Christian understanding of life after death. Many disciples of Christ are ignorant of their own tradition and would benefit immensely from knowing their own story clearly. But more specifically, it is only when we fix certain theological ideas like "life after death" in their proper place that we can understand this very crucial petition of the Prayer: "Thy will be done on earth as it is in heaven."

Let's begin with heaven.

Contrary to many well-meaning sermons and indeed even more funeral homilies, the Bible has very little interest in heaven. Strain the first five books of the Torah with a sieve that catches references to life after death and you'll have precious little for your efforts. That which happens in the grave is a very secondary consideration. For most of the authors of the Jewish faith, there is no expectation of an existence beyond the one lived out on earth. Human life is here and now. End of argument. When you die, there is nothing. From dust you were made and to dust you shall return.

Unlike modern self-help pop psychology, the Bible takes death very seriously. It is not a door to a better place. There is no alluring light that gets turned on when you expire. You don't walk from one joy to the next. You're dead and gone. Full stop.

Death is therefore the enemy. It is not a trifle to be brushed aside by a few platitudes and pastoral placebos. You see, there was no distinction between the body the soul . . . as if the latter could live on eternally while the former was as transitory as grass (Isa 40:7–8). Death was the end of the corporeal human and the spiritual human because they could never be conceived as separate. Indeed, this is still the "orthodox" Christian position though it is rarely expressed. From my perspective, it makes complete sense. Body and soul are essentially one even though we can speak of them as distinct and separate. Those who are pained in body often suffer in the soul as a consequence. The reverse is also true. Likewise, a spiritual illness manifests itself physically. So, death is the end. No spark, no flight of the soul.

"Doesn't the Bible mention heaven?" Is that your question?

Well, yes, heaven is raised, but it is largely God's abode. Angels are God's messengers, but there is no explicit idea that we will all somehow end up as one of these beings. Even though heaven is God's home, God seems bent upon spending most free time untangling the messes that human beings create on earth.

You'll find references to hell in the Jewish Scriptures. It's called "*Sheol.*" Don't imagine a little red-suited demon with horns and a pitch fork, sitting on a throne surrounded by fire and brimstone. *Sheol* is a dust heap where dead people go. Like the garbage bin in your computer, nothing happens there. There is no active agent doing anything to anyone in *Sheol*. It's a trash heap, a prison without a warden or guards, a place for spent beings. No judgment or guilt. No flames or torture. It's a dump, nothing more.

Moving to the Christian Scriptures, we will find a bit more interest in heaven. Yet, again, we will be misguided if we construe it to be a big idea. Jesus rarely mentions it. Like God, his gaze seems fixed on earth. Heaven can wait. If Jesus is pushed, as happens in a few references in John's gospel, he shows no strong desire to describe whatever God might have in store beyond the grave. Jesus employs a few metaphors about mansions in the sky. But generally, his message is to respond to those who look for heavenly signs and signals to be patient and keep your eyes on the real game. It's down here and it's right now.

It is true. You can find plenty of material in the Christian Scriptures that appears to point to life beyond the veil. But I would caution that if you don't know the basic frame of reference of certain ideas and words, you will misunderstand both their import and importance.

What is Resurrection?

Take "resurrection" as a key doctrine.

Most Christians hear it as a promise of a personal salvation constituting life after death. We say to ourselves that resurrection is the promise that when I die, "I will see Gramma again." Isn't that why Jesus died and rose from the dead? Didn't he suffer the pain of the cross and rise from the empty tomb so that the elect can all get into heaven? Surely that is the central message of the Christian story of resurrection! Redeemed and restored as heavenly spirits, we will enjoy an eternity with our Creator. It's a beautiful picture that has considerable weight in our liturgical tradition.

But this mythology of eternal life in heaven has very little to do with the original notion of "resurrection." Let's go back in history to explore the principles behind resurrection.

First, we'll need to appreciate the basic theological formula that was used as the interpretive key to righteous living. The Hebraic mind understood human life as a reflection of God's judgment. There was no other way to weigh God's relative perspective on human virtue. You had to weigh God's favor or disfavor by the circumstances of a believer's life. Those who enjoyed good health were obviously blessed by God. Those who suffered illness and distress were being punished for sin.

Of course, no one wants to suffer needlessly. So, there was considerable effort put into shaping a righteous existence. Remember, there is no afterlife in which to make amends. It was now or nothing. Your duty was to live a just, faith-filled life, keep God close, avoid any dalliance with other idols or deities. Your ambition was to live justice and love mercy, and walk humbly with God (Mic 6:8).

And if one's life followed these three simple steps, God would confer wholeness and well-being. Simply put: do good and God blesses you. Do evil and you get punished!

The people who lived well were doing so because they were righteous, keeping God's commandments and living within the requirements of the covenant. God favored them and their actions. It goes without saying that those who were suffering, were tortured because they were evildoers—having denied God in some fashion.

It's a simple and very convincing theological formula. Indeed, we still often make reference to it. When fortune shines on us unexpectedly, we say, "I don't know what I have done to deserve this!"

Now, there is problem with this line of reasoning if you are a small nation in the wrong place at the wrong time. If you and your country happen to be the doormat to every imperial ambition, you're going to feel constantly guilty and sinful. You are going to suffer continual doubt and distress because you are constantly being punished by invading armies. The land of Palestine was the land bridge between many competing nations and continents. Its geographical position meant it would be the battleground for empires. How could they escape the ravages of war, and therefore, how could they ever feel blessed by God since it appeared *God* was constantly punishing them with the ravages of war?

As one prophet succeeded another, the people became convinced that they could never become righteous enough to convince God that they had turned from their evil ways. What was the solution to this seemingly impossible trap of theological flagellation?

That which appeared on the horizon was the dream that eventually God would step into history to hold back marauding nations. If the people of God would be patient, there would come a day of reckoning. Call it the final chapter, the last battle, or as the Bible says, "the Day of the Lord," the principle was the same. Eventually, all nations would relinquish their evil ways and find peace in praising the God of Israel (Ps 96, 99). They would forsake the idolatry of power and come to the mountain of the Lord and live by the law. Sprinkled throughout the Psalms and the prophets (Mic 4:3) is the expectation that this day of judgment would happen within our history and be a visible and tangible "correction" of past injustices visited upon God's chosen people. So much for theology.

In the second century before the common era, Antiochus IV, a weak leader of the crumbling Persian Empire,[1] tried to reinforce his power over Palestine by forcing the Judeans to renounce their historic faith. With these public conversions, he hoped to achieve political cohesion and obedience.

To make concrete this legally required religious uniformity, the leaders of the Judeans were forced to renounce their trust in God in full view of the gathered people. Then they were forced to eat pork while the crowds

1. Crossan, *God and Empire*, 184.

watched. The leaders were trooped out first and shown this literal meal of humble pie.

Many refused. They would rather die than deny their trust in the God of Israel, the God of justice and mercy. For their obstinacy, they were tortured horribly before the onlookers. It must have been a horrific desecration, for it was branded on the consciousness of the people as the ultimate injustice. Bodies were torn apart, lives horribly lost—all to retain righteousness.[2]

You can see what is coming, can't you? This horrendous pain and suffering runs contrary to the well-accepted theology of God's righteousness. If God blesses those who are faithful, how could God allow these spiritual heroes to be tortured precisely because they remained faithful? It's impossible, it's not supposed to work that way! Generations of theology tell us the exact opposite. Even while the tortured bodies were taken and disposed of with no ceremony, people still cried out. Surely God would not allow this injustice to stand for very long! These mutilated bodies would need to be restored. When God began to rule on earth and initiate the event of the great reckoning, how could God ignore the martyrs of the faith who had given their bodies to show their devotion?

Before the justice of God could be visible to the nations, these unjustly tortured bodies needed to be restored to wholeness and life—they needed to be resurrected.

Resurrection was therefore not originally a code word for spiritual renewal or the division of body and soul. Quite the contrary. Those who had been beaten, broken, and massacred for their faith would be restored in body and spirit down here on earth. These martyrs who had been held in *Sheol* would be brought back from death and given new life. The only vestige of this idea is found in the Apostles' Creed. When we recite the line about Jesus as a savior who ". . . was crucified, dead and buried," we add: "He descended into hell. On the third day, he rose . . . ." The descent into hell, known as the "harrowing of hell," was the event in which Jesus went "down" to break the bonds of that relentless jail and brought back the tortured martyrs. When he rose, it was after having freed the unjustly tortured faithful ones.

2. This was the instigation for the revolt of Maccabees and it was on the basis of the resistance of these martyrs that the Hebraic state of Israel enjoyed relative independence for a century before the Romans took over.

The resurrection of the faithful was presumed to be a signal of God's coming reign on earth. Since God would restore the martyrs' bodies first, once we saw resurrected bodies, or indeed the resurrection of Jesus, we can presume that God's judgement of the nations has begun. Crossan calls this "God's Big Cleanup."[3] The Gospels are a witness to the fact that God is coming soon to establish God's will here on earth.

Is There Life before Death?

The weight of all this history and hope is captured by the simple line, "Thy will be done on earth as it is in heaven." We are unwittingly praying for the day of judgement to arrive. Jesus began the process. As Paul suggests in his first letter to the church in Corinth, his resurrection is like the first fruits of an autumn fall harvest (1 Cor 15:20). A few individual fruits appear as the signal and testimony that more, much more, is to come. The resurrection of Jesus is the evidence that God's will *is* come to earth and that it will now take over.

Recall again the "performative" language of the prayer and we now readjust our picture of that first community of people "on the way" making a statement about life *before* death. Their eyes were fixed on the earth and they were proclaiming a fact that by common consent they were allowed to direct and shape their reality. They were a company of people who lived in God's realm, for it is coming now.

A king was a king because the king's word and will were law. The people acknowledged its prominence and power. There was no other option. And let's be clear. At the time when the Prayer was first used, there was no halfway thinking. You couldn't have a little bit of monarchical authority, a small taste of "Lordship," as if you could follow the king's rule on even days and your own on the odd days. It was all or nothing.

"Your will be done." It was a statement of fact. For these followers of Jesus, there was a sun shining in the blue sky, water flowing in the oceans, and God's will reigning on earth.

Can you imagine the power of their collective will? Incredible and unchanging. I can conceive of no other source for their courage and determination.

Nevertheless, I realize that at this stage it appears that all we have are words. Noble words, but just words nonetheless. They have little authority

3. Crossan, *God and Empire*, 183–87.

unless they are lived out in some concrete fashion. The first followers of Jesus were no more gullible than moderns. If there had been no transformed reality that corresponded to the one which their words described, the whole project would have been either wishful thinking or dangerous self-deception. As we move through the Prayer we will be able to understand how God's will was seen to be lived out.

To be sure, the Lord's Prayer contains its own answer to the nature of the first community of Jesus. And it is on the basis of the picture we can hear by listening between the lines of this ancient prayer that we can build a picture of the beauty and attractiveness of "the way." But let us leave that for a few more chapters.

Currently, let a simple fact settle into our frame of reference for the tradition we call "Christianity": it is a *materialist religion*. We are in the business of transforming this real, material world. We can take off in flights of fancy of course, but our chief responsibility is the recreating of this earth as a place where God's principles and purpose will reign.

Heaven Is Just Fine!

As I mentioned, the Prayer is itself not particularly concerned with heaven or life after death. At least that would not be the first and primary implication of this portion of the Prayer. Heaven seems to be the place where God's will reigns without interruption or disruption. Heaven is doing just fine, thank you very much. That's not where Jesus points his disciples. Don't get distracted by the allure of a perfect place somewhere else. Our work is here on earth. That's where God's will is living and growing.

We can hear this affirmation as a rather simplistic reorienting of the disciples' perspective or as a profound pastoral and theological affirmation. I prefer the latter explanation. When I am asked about life after death, I can quote Scripture and I often make reference to Paul's Letter to the Romans in which he states that love is stronger than death (Rom 8:31). He is right. Our first answer to the problem of death is love.

One of my favorite university lectures is the one in which I broach the question of love's power. I start by asking if anyone has a loving mother. A sea of hands goes up. I choose an eager student in the front row and ask, "How do you know?" They often reply that they just do. It's not up for debate, they are absolutely convinced of their mother's love.

I press a little harder. "But your mom is not here; how do you know she still loves you?" What a ridiculous question! And after the laughter subsides, and we get serious again, I hear all the firm, almost offended protests:

"She doesn't have to be in the room for me to be sure of it."

"Mom has never stopped loving me!"

"Mom tells me every time she sees me! I don't need her to be right here to know that. It's a fact."

Having proved that love is not governed by geography, I move on to the question of chronology. "When was the last time you saw your mom?" The answer is usually vague: a month or two, sometime in the summer. It's the start of classes after all and no self-respecting university student would admit to regular contact with a parent in front of their peers. I suggest that if it's been so long, how can anyone possibly be convinced of their mother's love? "Maybe she has forgotten you?" Well, that raises hackles of indignation. An intelligent kid in the back row shouts out, "A mother's love is not diminished by time."

I rest my case.

Love is not governed by space or time. Do we think death will therefore change anything? Of course not! Love is more powerful than the grave. Paul was right when he argued that we are never separated from those who love us.

Jesus makes a slightly different affirmation and I find it equally satisfying. It's implicit in this line of his Prayer, which affirms that in heaven God's will reigns. Another way of thinking about this line is to say that heaven, that existence that lies beyond or above or between the moments of this life, is in God's hand. If God is who we claim God is, then there is no need to worry. Whatever happens beyond the grave, God has it covered. I can trust that One who made me in love will have planned well. I will not be lost because the love that shaped me from my beginning will be with me in my ending. The One whose will reigns "in heaven" has my welfare in hand . . . even, and especially, for my life beyond the grave. Enough said.

Let's get back to earth. God's heaven will take care of itself.

Two Wills of God

There is usually an enlightened moment during the process of grieving that we raise this line from the Prayer as an answer to the inconsistent or unjust nature of human existence. At Frank's funeral, I heard it employed several times as we lined up for the refreshments. People would turn to each other and admit reverently that it "was God's will." That seemed to answer all questions and still the storm of regret that we all felt.

The theory is easy enough to understand on many levels. Theologically, we are admitting that God holds all the cards. In the end, God gives and God takes away according to God's desires. There is nothing we can do but let go of our attempts to control our destinies and admit that we are simply along for the ride. "God's will *will* be done." After all, if you are the Creator of the Universe, you should have some "right," if not some considerable responsibility, to be in charge. Life and death are God's to give. End of argument. Pass me the sandwiches.

On an emotional level, this phrase allows me to fail. There are moments when I need not be strong. Do you ever feel that way? After a week of strenuous effort, there comes a moment when it is healthy and important to admit that we can't change history. There are people and practices, programs and projects that are beyond us. No matter how anxious we might become or how deeply we might yearn to make a difference, we can't. It is this impossibility that we admit when we mouth the words, "Thy will be done." There is a great deal that is beyond our control as human beings. We are victims of random events, some tragic like the death of a young man like Frank and some quite delightful like falling in love. Whether it's darkness or light, there is much that is beyond our abilities and the Prayer helps us to be honest about our frail natures. Thank God!

On a more subtle, spiritual level, this phrase is a relinquishment of our pretense to be immortal and all-powerful. In that instance, it acts as a very healthy corrective to the human sin of pride. After all our boasting and strutting, there is a very sobering fact we all must accept: we will die. All of us. No one gets out of this world alive. There is no way to avoid it. I say to my university students that it is the only significant act that they and every human being will achieve perfectly. Just wait long enough and it will happen. Put less cynically, this phrase acts as a reminder that we are not our own makers. The One who shaped us from dust will eventually bring us home, return us to that from which we came. In the end, it is a phrase that comforts us deeply for in it we recognize the truth. We are not alone. The One who made us in love will never forsake us.

But (in theology there is always a "but!"), there is more to be said about this phrase. It is not enough to relinquish control to God. I respect those who find the peace in this humility of spirit and I wish I had the capacity to reach that level of communion and trust with my Maker. But, the phrase "Thy will be done on earth as it is in heaven" can also be an invitation to active participation in the reign of God.

Picture a king reigning over a territory. There is an unspoken acceptance that a monarch's will is law. His decrees are unquestionable and we all accept that his words hold the power to change our common purpose and dreams. Nevertheless, we also recognize that the king's will is useless without the active assistance of his subjects. The king has little direct control separate from the agency of the citizens of his realm. Without our hands, how will the king build a new world? Without our hearts, how will the king's deep love be known? Likewise, not all the king's projects or purposes are hidden. There are usually some pretty clear overtones and expectations of the king. The subjects of a kingdom align themselves with these basic principles. The same is true of the kingdom of God. God's rule on earth will have power in direct proportion to the willingness and courage of those who pray God's presence into existence.

Recite with me please: "Thy kingdom come and thy will be done on earth as it is in heaven." Let's repeat it. "Thy kingdom come and thy will be done on earth as it is in heaven."

What do you feel?

Of course, we notice that our hearts are at repose, resting in a peaceful state where we relinquish our grasping natures. We *can* let go. This is precisely the first step of embodying God's reign—making it real. The next step is to take a deep breath and gather up our energies, for we have now committed ourselves to be active citizens in God's realm. It is not enough to let God do it. How will this happen without our active cooperation?

It can't.

One last note. We have recognized that the realm of God is not a future waiting beyond death. It is a present-day reality. Each Sunday when we recite this prayer, we invoke God's reign right here and right now. What follows in the rest of the Prayer is a description of the key points that constitute this every day kingdom. Contrary to your expectations, the program for this king's rule is very concrete and clear. It is not an impossible dream, but a very pragmatic political and social program. It has three key components: Bread for today. No debt for tomorrow. Peace through justice. We will dedicate each of the next three chapters to look at each of these components in turn.

7

A Social Program: "Give us this day . . ."

Bread Day

I AM A SHAMELESS BAKER.

I'll make bread everywhere for anyone. It has become my vocation. I am no longer just a pastor of religion. In Cuba, they call me the *"panadero"* pastor . . . the baker pastor. They know me too well.

Ask me to teach and I'll bring along my bread bowl. A case in point: as I edit this chapter, I am in the middle of making pita bread for a class in pastoral theology. I have used bread-making for everything from examining the complexity of biomedical ethics to instructing vacation Bible school. It works as a form of prayer and I have lost count how many times I have employed it as the basis for a lecture on life and hope. Bread-making is an all-purpose pedagogical tool.

Likewise, bread goes well with preaching. Even if people don't like listening, at least the show of making a batch of buns before their very eyes has entertainment value. No one goes to sleep during bread-making sermons. Better still, make bread and pass it out while you preach. There's nothing like the taste of fresh bread to reinforce preaching about the love of our Creator.

Bread also happens to be multilingual. If you can't speak French or German or Spanish, I am living testimony to the fact that if you can make bread, you can communicate very well. Bread contains a message that everyone understands. Even if you don't know a single word in another language, make people some fresh bread, share it, and you will immediately convey a depth of meaning that most linguistic students will spend years trying to achieve.

Beyond teaching, preaching, and general communication, bread-making has been a very important ministry. Let me tell you the story of Bread Day.

Bread Day began when I started to explore the many gifts I had been given as the leader of a church. There are many fringe benefits to ministry that we take for granted: the compassion and care of a large and growing family, the invitation to be present at the hinge moments in another person's life, and the enthusiasm of joining in a common purpose to transform the world. Those are just a few of the fringes.

There are many "fridge" benefits too: mountains of homemade cookies, bottomless cups of coffee, and bread . . . lots of bread.

At first, we didn't know what we were doing when we talked about taking all the great food we enjoyed as a church and giving it away to the wider community. My national church had asked local congregations to reach beyond predictable constituencies, so we devised a plan to make and bake bread to share. We didn't realize it until after we had done a few bread days that we were actually making "daily bread." Free and fresh, bread for the world.

That was our vision.

We gather at 7 AM and begin the many batches of dough. Each one makes 115 buns, and we will eventually shape them into rounds of seven buns each. If we have enough mixers, we'll prepare twenty-five batches.

Down at the far counter you can see a retired school principal, a practicing dermatologist, a man on income assistance, and an unemployed heavy machinery operator. They all come from the church; some belong to the street crowd that grace our building on Saturday night and others from the pews. They're up to their elbows in flour, making food to share—a metaphor of God's reign.

Turn to opposite end of the kitchen and you'll see a retired nurse and a practicing one. They're buttering the pans we will use for baking—quite a pile is stacked already. It's greasy, noisy work. So, they speak loudly. Today it's birthing jokes.

Out in the parking lot, the oven has arrived. A special treat for this Bread Day, the Speerville Organic Flour Mill from up river has brought down their wood-fired beauty: an oven that bakes twenty loaves at a time in just over twelve minutes—the power of a unique ecological design.

Another team is putting out tables in the gym to hold trays of rising buns and the cooling racks for baked ones. We have a supply of bags, and a one-sheet flier that explains Daily Bread and invites people to share their bread with their circle.

As the bread bakes, they do just that. First, people from the street come in—they're broke and have nothing to eat; the smell of baking bread has drawn them to the church like bees to honey. Taking a bun in their hands, it's like a miracle. Later in the day, the church elders arrive. They are wanting to drop off buns for older folks who are shut in. One elder returns to tell me that for years he had been trying to get a senior widow to open the door and at least exchange greetings. She had never once opened her door, until he showed up at her door with fresh bread. Now she flings the door wide open; "Fresh bread!" she exclaims. "Please come in and share it with me." It seems bread is also a universal key. It opens doors long shut tight.

Once, we had bread going to both sides of a serious labor dispute. We didn't organize that one. We're modest about our bread-making, but the fact that the two sides soon came to an agreement . . . well, we like to think God works through bread in mysterious ways.

As the day passes and word spreads down the street, more strangers come and sheepishly ask if they can have some buns, even though they have no way to pay. I recall one person in particular. He's been to the church before: a good fellow who lost his job when the restaurant where he worked as a sous chef closed. He hasn't been able to find work since, and it's been very tough to feed his five children. Welfare doesn't come close to being enough. He doesn't want to have to beg. It's soul-destroying. But this is not begging. This bread is taken by everyone: rich and poor. No one pays. After I explain that fact, I can see the light rise in their eyes. At the persistence of the team giving out the loaves, he gathers up six rounds for his large family. "Bless you, the kids will love this," he whispers as he leaves with a smile and a bit more dignity.

On Bread Day, there are always surprises—a few stories to reassure us we are on the right track. This day is no exception. One round of buns made it to the doorstep of a neighbor of a church member. This person was a very busy gynecologist who hardly had time to pack snacks for her kids' lunches—let alone bake bread. She opened the door, looked at the proffered rounds of steaming buns, heard the explanation of free bread from a community of faith, and blurted out, "What kind of church are you people?"

As we clean and close up, Becky, a young university student, comes to me. She had volunteered to help out so she could witness "what you Christians do." She is part of a coven from the Wicca spiritual tradition. She is also a vocal lesbian. For those two reasons, she felt she would never be welcome in a church building, let alone invited into active participation. After a full day of baking and distributing bread, Becky smiles from ear to ear and says, "This is so cool. If only all Christians were like this."

Bread Day has become a living gospel.

I think I must be the only minister in the country who regularly has parishioners come up to him, clap me on the back, and say, "Your buns are great." Another fringe benefit to ministry.

"Give Us This Day . . ."

Bread Day was planned as a means for living out our obligations as a community of faith, but it very soon became apparent to us that we had stumbled on a central truth of the Prayer. The "daily bread" of which Jesus was speaking was not initially spiritual. He knew the power of real bread, fresh bread, given away freely. Of course, there are spiritual characteristics of shared bread, but they are often secondary to the very material, alluring qualities of fresh bread.

There is no doubt that this petition had captured the imagination of generations and enjoys a tremendous cultural recognition. Even if people do not practice Christianity, they have heard about "daily bread."

I want to suggest that it is the building block, both figuratively and literally, of the kingdom of God that the community of faith constitutes every time they pray this prayer.

In a phrase: the kingdom of God is known through sharing daily bread. Clearly Luke makes this assertion in the story of Emmaus (Luke 24:13–35), with which he concludes his Gospel. Do you recall it? It's Easter morning, there are hints of resurrection in the air. We are told that two people are out on a journey to Emmaus, a town seven miles from Jerusalem. Jesus joins them on their pilgrimage, but they do not know him. He opens their eyes to the reason for his crucifixion and they are entranced. They do not know him to be their Savior until he breaks bread with them. Apart from the obvious suggestion that the "Way" to follow Jesus is to get out on the road, Luke makes it clear that Jesus comes alive when we share bread with strangers.

Of course, one could construe the "daily bread" we ask to receive in the Prayer as food for the soul. I would not want to deny that many people recite the Prayer and come to this sentence hoping to feel the heartwarming soul food and comfort of their Savior. They have no need for actual bread. Indeed, they have too much real bread. Their deep desire is for spiritual sustenance: something to get through the week.

All our spiritual needs notwithstanding, the Prayer is first and foremost about real bread. Perhaps if we back up and examine where the idea arises, it will become clear how "daily bread" is both a material and miraculous gift of God.

One of the techniques I use for bread-making as a teaching tool is to invite participants to name the number of breads described in the Bible. The first answer is usually, "daily bread." It sticks out as a primary category. If I push, people will come up with the five small loaves from the story of the feeding of the multitudes. Then there's the barley loaves of John's gospel. Reaching back further, someone will try: "unleavened bread." It is the liberation bread that the chosen people, enslaved by Egyptians, grabbed as they ran out the door on their escape to freedom. Once we are at the Exodus, the next suggestion is: "Bread of heaven, manna."

That's what I have been hoping to hear. So, I reply and ask, "what is the chief characteristic of manna?" You have to picture me making bread as we speak, so I have their complete attention—they want to learn. They start guessing:

"It's sweet."

"It fell from heaven."

"It's God's gift."

"It's reliable."

Let's begin with the basics: manna was a bread that was given to the people by God so they would not starve in the wilderness. It is therefore real bread that sustains us physically. There is a spiritual dimension—the sensation of abundance—but it begins as a necessary food staple. Manna is a gift in the wilderness and not used as a means of economic exploitation. No one makes money from manna. It is God's gift to people who are lost in the desert and have nothing more to live by except their trust in their Creator.

Manna had a peculiar distributive quality. It fell each day and there was enough for everyone. You had to go and gather up your portion. But if you tried to take more than your share, it would spoil. There was no way to accumulate advantage or surplus. So, there we have it. Manna was the great equalizer. Its two chief characteristics: it's free and it's enough.

The kingdom of God begins when people have food without price and enjoy a sufficient supply every day. That's its positive expression. To put it negatively: praying for daily bread means no one starves, no one makes their fortune on the basis of basic human needs like bread, and no one is excluded from God's table because they can't pay. If that makes "daily bread" sound like the beginning of a political program, then you understand it well. That is precisely the right tone that Jesus was capturing in this simple petition. This is God's political program for a concrete and very practical community.

Here's how the first disciples actually accomplished the feat of creating just such a community of daily bread. Imagine people who are hungry. We're back to the context of scarcity. There are no shopping malls, no massive bakeries. Bread was a daily problem to solve and it was not easy. If you were a peasant without land, it was a question of finding someone to hire you so eventually you would have a little spare change to buy bread from a larger household. Tough times. Now picture people who commit themselves to gather regularly and bring and share everything they have. Imagine these people doing this "share" meal often enough that it is *more* than a ceremony. It was a means of mutual support and sustenance.

Any Christian will affirm that they have witnessed the miracle of abundance in a church potluck dinner. When people share what they have, there is always more than enough. I have yet to be part of a potluck that didn't work its magic of abundance. Sometimes we have too many sweets or an excess of potato salad, but the basic principle is a no-brainer. Share everything and no one will go hungry.

Reading between the lines of the multiple stories of the feeding of the multitudes, we see this miracle of abundance taking place. It is only John's gospel that turns the multiplication of loaves into a "sign" of Christ's power (John 6:14). When this tale is reduced to a show of divinely sent potency wielded by Jesus, it loses its actual authority. It's a nice story of Christ, and it is perhaps reassuring to know he has God's gift of creating something from nothing. But surely this story is not about Jesus' power. Rather it is the early church speaking of its own miracle: how, when the people gather with Jesus or in his name and the bread is passed around, there is plenty to eat. That seems to be the point of Mark's recounting of the feeding of the multitude, not once but twice (Mark 8:18–21). Hungry people who trust in God, who share their bread, are always fed. Indeed, they enjoy a great, overflowing abundance.

This is the first miracle of daily bread: it embodies and conveys the wonder of abundance. It is breathtaking to recognize that when the first community asked for daily bread, they were not sitting on their hands and hoping God would perform wilderness magic. They knew the petition of daily bread was an invitation to form the "share community." It was a statement of commitment to make abundance a reality.

Now, how about the most important question of this book? Take a deep breath. Get yourself ready for the obvious and most exacting query.

Why don't modern Christians do the same thing as their ancestors? Why do we not share daily bread?

It's not too much of a stretch to consider the church becoming the company of free bread. Imagine if the people looked on the church as a place where you could always get food for today—not as a charitable program reserved for the "deserving," but as a matter of course. Take the gyms we don't use any more and turn them into bakeries. Buy the flour, gather the community of mixers, and start producing daily bread.

Then give it away. No questions asked. Everyone needs bread, so we give it away to any and all who ask for it. It's fresh! Who wouldn't want some? How many loaves would we have to give out before people would begin to ask: "What kind of church is this?" How many Bread Days would we have to live out before we were changed into God's reign here on earth?

Take it step further and ask why bread isn't free in the wider society. As a modern, developed community, we have decided that economic considerations are not an obstacle to receiving essential services. In many countries, medical care is offered on the basis of need. Likewise, we structure elementary educational programs as a right for all. There is no price to pay for going to the first steps of education.

Why not food? What if bread were free? In Cuba, one bun a day is a "right" for every citizen. It is priced at a penny a piece, essentially free. Likewise, milk for children is subsidized to the extent that it is without price, for all intents and purposes.

What is the matter with extracting food from our system of financial gain? Let it be sold at prices that reflect fair prices for producers, but let there be no profiteering in bread. Let this step of making bread free be the first essential real and symbolic step in "making poverty history."

Of course, there are many dimensions to making bread free. You will begin to name the downsides: economic distress, black market corruption, individual lethargy—but these kinds of complications are always part of the process of social change. We picture all the companies that will suffer because of a loss of revenue if a foodstuff like bread is made free. We picture people losing jobs when the profit motive is taken out of food. Yes, there are many legitimate objections.

Turn back the clock several centuries and it is remarkable how often the same arguments were made *against* the abolition of the slave trade. To many, it seemed both an impossible and an impractical dream to eliminate slavery. We now look at their objections and cry out, "How shortsighted and cowardly!"

Let that not be said of this generation.

If the first miracle of shared bread is "abundance," the very real satisfaction of living with food security, daily bread, a second miracle, can be characterized as "acceptance."

A Parable of Abundance and Acceptance

When my father was eighty-four, he asked if we could take a cross-country trip together. He wanted to visit the churches where he had passed his ministry for one last time. It took five days to cross from the forests of the province of Ontario to the flat plains of Saskatchewan. Canada is a big country, after all.

I eagerly agreed to the journey, because, from my youth, I had heard of the many little towns and small parishes through which we would pass. One, Landis, shone like a beacon of paradise. I recall how many times my dad would speak with affection about this small prairie town. "So flat you could see forever. Not a single tree or hill to get in the way of the view."

In the five days of that car ride, I came to know a man who had never been very present in my father. He related extraordinary stories of his main pastorates: parishioners with loaded pistols, suicide attempts aborted at the last minute, split-second marriages . . . amazing. But there was one story that trumped all the rest. It happened on day three of our trip.

As we broke through the boreal forest of the pre-Cambrian shield in northern Ontario and started to drive out on the plains that stretch for a thousand miles towards the Rocky Mountains, my Dad blurted out: "Stop the car!"

It was so unlike him and so abrupt that I thought we must have hit an animal or that his wallet had flown out the window he had opened. "Stop the car!"

And I did, quickly.

Once we were pulled over to the side of the road, I looked at him questioningly. "What?"

He said nothing, but deliberately and slowly opened his door and stepped out. Thinking he might need help, I got out of my side and came around to him. He was staring off to the west, the prairie stretched out as far as the eye could see. He took a deep breath and said solemnly, "I'm home."

"Home? How could you be home? You barely spent three years out here! Apart from that, your entire life was spent building a home in the east."

Dad got back in the car, smiling. He then told me a story I had never heard before: the tale of his shining moment. Everyone has such an event in their life. It is the singular event or period of time that captures your essence. The time when the stars were aligned and you soared like a meteor.

My dad's special time happened in that little town, Landis. He and Mom travelled out to this hamlet directly from Princeton, New Jersey, where my father had finished a Masters in Theology on the subject of Søren Kierkegaard. Princeton was the center of scholasticism. Albert Einstein lived literally two doors away.

When he arrived at this wind-swept town, he thought he was as far from the real world—that is to say the world of ideas and philosophy—as he could possibly get. He told me of walking toward the church, seeing a man in overalls with his head in a broken tractor, and saying to himself, "Well, son, you are now definitely lost in the beyond of the beyond."

But what my father discovered was that the man fixing the farm machinery was an expert in educational systems and pedagogical theory. The newly elected socialist government of the province would regularly arrive at this man's farm for think-tank planning sessions. My dad would preach in the morning, his ideas would be discussed in the afternoon by the provincial cabinet, and become the foundation for developing legislation on Monday. Ideas mattered. There was no glib theology allowed. You were tested. I can picture my dad rising to the challenge of making his thoughts concrete and acceptable enough to stand the close scrutiny of his political friends who waited around the kitchen table on those Sunday afternoons.

A time like no other in Canada. It was from that very Saskatchewan government that the germ of public and universal health care arose. Long-held paradigms changed seemingly overnight.

It was probably from this place, where values mattered so much, that my dad had the dream to finish a doctorate. At that time, money was always a problem. So, when an eastern church invited him to come and be their second minister while doing his studies at the same time, he jumped at the chance. His idea had been to get the doctorate and then return out west to continue in his ministry.

Yet no sooner had he arrived, than the "senior" minister (to whom he was to be more like a son than a colleague) had serious heart failure. Dad was drafted into double the workload and the doctorate was put on hold.

The work was not what he expected at all. Out west, he had been engaged in everything from high-level provincial politics to grassroots community leadership. Exciting and fulfilling. In Toronto, he was expected to be a kind of soul servant, cleaning up spiritual messes for patrons who couldn't (or wouldn't) see their minister in any other light. Dad grew depressed.

My mom, seeing my father's distress, made a plan. Even though she was eight months pregnant with me, she went out and bought a round-trip ticket to Landis and gave it to my dad at the dinner table. "Here," she said, "Go home." He did not hesitate.

The next day, my father was on the train headed for the west—a two-day trip. Landis was on the mainline from the capital of Saskatchewan to the border with Alberta, but it was too small a town to have twenty-four–hour staff. The train wouldn't stop there unless someone, usually Jake (the station master), hung out a lamp to signal the engineer to stop the train.

My dad called Jake from Winnipeg and asked if he could perform that essential task. "Sure, Vic," Jake replied, as if he had been talking to his pastor every day in the three intervening years since they had last seen each other.

It was late when Dad's trip was coming to an end. The train raced through the darkened field. In those days, no one wasted electricity on night-lights. The train rounded the final curve toward the station platform of Landis. He was so excited that he could hardly stop his hands from shaking as he pulled down his suitcases and made for the door.

As he got to the door, he saw it!

It wasn't just a single light, but *hundreds* that were turned on to signal the train: cars lights, lanterns, kitchen candles, etc. Jake had apparently told the community that Vic was coming home and everyone had come out to welcome him back. The prodigal pastor had returned. The party lasted for three days! Talk about breaking bread!

I was impressed by my dad's shining moment and wished that I could know what it would be like to have such a strong affinity with a people and place. I had moved around too often and done too many jobs to put down roots. It would not happen for me, I thought. About three months after I had delivered my dad back to his home in the east, I was on a journey to Cuba. I had been there often as a leader of a tour group. This time, I was coming early. As I stepped from the plane and could feel the heat and humidity, I stopped, took a deep breath, and said to myself, "I'm home."

There is no passion to compare with this feeling of being "home."

It is my only way to express the second miracle of shared bread in the Jesus movement. After the satisfaction of a filled stomach, the shared bread signaled that all are welcome and no one is excluded—it was key! A sensation of wonder and deep satisfaction. Now this acceptance in shared bread has a history that needs to be explained as a form of healing. There is a very important distinction to make between curing the disease and healing the illness. However, first we must understand the nature of sin in first-century Palestine.

Sin and Healing

We must again suspend our modern definitions in order to think our way back into a different world. We have to take away Western preoccupations with sex and what my Presbyterian preacher grandfather would call "the lusts of the flesh." All these pornographic, sensual, and alluring "sins" may appear as eternal examples of deadly shame. Add to them the things Christians lament every Sunday in their prayers of confession: things we have done or not done that cause pain in the heart of God, and we have a comprehensive definition. Are these not our sins? But let us use a small "s" for such matters. To use a medical metaphor, these are the ancillary, secondary sites of cancer. The primary source is much deeper. In the Christian world and indeed in the eyes of Jesus, "Sin" is of another order. Essentially there are of two kinds of Sin—both involve distance from God created by human pretense.

Human beings are anxious creatures and so we pretend. We pretend that we are not mortal, that we will not die, and that we are in charge of our coming and going. We pretend we are self-made and we can control all things around us. This is the Sin of pride. We pretend that we are a little less than God. In some instances, we pretend that we don't even need God.

At the other end of the scale is the pretense that we are little more than wild beasts. We have no purpose on this earth except as the lucky primates who currently sit at the top of the food chain. This life asks nothing of us and gives nothing in return. This is the Sin of sloth. We are pretending to be less than what God created. When I say "sloth," you think of dirty clothes left on the floor, teenagers who sit like lumps in front of the television, or perhaps a cute slow-moving mammal—but sloth is not about laziness. It is a spiritual crisis of imagination. We cannot picture ourselves as anything other than directionless animals.

Whether pride or sloth, Sin puts a distance between the Creator and the creature. We are no longer able to stand up and confront our Maker in our nakedness. Surely this is the meaning behind the betrayal of promise in the story of the expulsion from Eden, found in Genesis 3. It's not about sex or physical nudity. The woman and man cover their bodies because they feel vulnerable before God. They know there is no pretense, no real way to hide from God.

But we do try to pretend. From that time east of Eden, we become more and more imaginative in our mechanism of pretense: we invent games of power called war and violence. We constructed dens of apathy with names like casinos or brothels. From our Sin, so many other sins pour out. However, if we are to address the nasty "sins" of our culture, we must first uncover the "Sin" that beset us.

In the time of Jesus, it was presumed that one's life and physical condition gave evidence of one's relative merit or sinfulness. As I explained in the previous chapter, the theological formula went like this: live righteously and God will bless you. Act sinfully and God will curse you.

So, as the disciples argue in John's gospel (John 9:1), a person's blindness is evidence that someone sinned. Either the person who is blind or his immediate family. The condition is irrefutable evidence of sin. Since there was no division of body and spirit, a physical condition like leprosy was also seen as a spiritual problem. Likewise, other physical ailments were deemed to be evidence of unrighteousness and therefore to be considered as contamination: issues of bodily fluids, any form of physical disfigurement, or skin disease. Those who worked in secondary contaminating circumstances: prostitutes and those who handled the dead . . . they were also sinful. As tertiary sins, people who worked overtly contrary to God's will were also considered sinful: tax collectors who lived from the injustice of collaborating with the occupying forces and anyone who had commerce with Gentiles. Not right and therefore not righteous.

Next step: contamination. Sin is not static in this world. It is contagious. Imagine a leper living in a family compound. He is sinful because his disease shows it clearly. With continued and intimate contact, others of his circle will also contract leprosy. What other conclusion can we draw except that sin is contagious? You can catch it.

So, the best medical advice and spiritual common sense of the day prescribed segregation as the best, and in some cases only, solution. Lepers lived apart in colonies of fellow lepers. Menstruating women ate and slept in the now infamous "red tent." Tax collectors kept to themselves (Luke 5:29). Prostitutes even more so.

Let us not see this initially as oppression. It was tough medicine, but it was accepted as the best one could hope for. You didn't want to pass your sin on to someone else, so you kept your distance out of respect and compassion for the healthy.

It was just medical common sense. The reigning wisdom spoke volumes. After generations of experimentation and experience, it was accepted as obvious that a single sinner could infect a healthy family. Put a prostitute amongst the synagogue Pharisees and they *would* catch her sin and be ritually unclean. Contact with a tax collector or a man bleeding by the side of the road would certainly contaminate them and therefore disqualify them from performing their functions in Jerusalem.[1]

Now, let us turn to the kingdom movement of Jesus. Have you ever noticed that there is a singular complaint leveled at him? The gossip gallery is active and always present at the edge of the Gospels, mumbling and wringing their hands. They don't ever say Jesus speaks for too long. No problems with his theological arguments. It's not body odor, harsh language, or family dynamics that sends them into fits of frustration. The one and only criticism is that Jesus eats with sinners and publicans. It is his table

1. The story of the Good Samaritan (Luke 10:25–37) is an example of priests wanting to avoid contamination and therefore "passing by on the other side," except—and this is the hinge point of the story—the priest and Levite were travelling from Jerusalem to Jericho. Obviously, their work day was done and so they could have stopped without putting in jeopardy their sacramental efficacy. Luke's reversal of meaning is made more obvious. The Judean leaders could have stopped, but it was a heretic, a Samaritan, who risked contamination out of compassion.

fellowship that is so problematic! It's not the timing of his dinners. There is no criticism of drunkenness or debauchery. Gluttony is not an issue. It is the simple act of breaking bread with contaminated people.

Why? Why does it matter with whom Jesus shares his meals?

First, let us recognize that the dinner table is where all the important actions take place. When they recline at table, the Judeans, particularly, and the people of the Mediterranean in general are risking a great deal: their personal security, their emotional privacy and spiritual righteousness. When you stumble upon a meal scene in Mark or Luke, you should see it as a key story. The stakes have just been raised. In sharing food, we expose ourselves to others: they see our basic humanness and our need for nourishment. This is the reason that meals are often employed as the "seal" on a covenant. You only eat when you have or want to create common security.

The centrality of meal fellowship, as symbol and enactment of community, is made all the more visible by common dishes. There are no discrete portions. You have no personal plate or utensils. All food is served on a single platter and everyone reaches in with their right hand or a piece of bread and scoops out what they wish. Put bluntly, your neighbor will have his hand in your food. In that case, you will be very picky about who reclines at meals beside you.

Now, picture Jesus. He's a religious authority, one who many people see on the same level as John the Baptizer. A local hero, the rock star that rises from home gigs in local bars to playing on the international stage. He's a somebody! Instead of sticking to the script and living within the well-prescribed limits of his renowned position and fame, he breaks entirely with accepted custom and common sense. He eats with contaminating sinners, collaborators, nobodies, and heretics. Not only will he get sick, he will lead all his disciples into contagion. He is spreading disease for no good reason. Imagine if Jesus had a virulent form of tuberculosis and he continued to work in pre-school programs, coughing on little kids every day. We'd call him not only irresponsible, but downright criminal! A dangerous, unthinking buffoon. If you can feel the frustration and dismay of someone running roughshod over our medical principles, then you have captured the mindset of the first-century southern Galilean gossip gallery. Jesus is a scandal!

On a deeper level, his bread-breaking practices are undermining the power of the elite. Obviously, some religious leaders felt a specific sting: Herod, the high priestly castes. But the problem was more widespread than individual invective. Jesus was laying down a foundation for a different community life and rule. Those who were really sensitive to, and cognizant of, the implications of his program (and let us grant that there were many individuals in first-century Palestine who were as intelligent if not more so than people 2,000 years later) could see where this was headed. Jesus was breaking away from trusted religious authority. He was rewriting the book of righteousness, and like the Pharisees he was placing power back in the hands of the people.

The Romans had no real interest in theological problems. I cannot picture the high priest going to Pilate and asking him to get rid of the Galilean preacher because he was ruining table etiquette and claiming the special religious authority so as to forgive sins. Pilate would have laughed and suggested that when you have a theological enemy you use back alleys and hidden knives to the solve that kind of problem.[2] If, however, Jesus is setting up a different social order, one that took no notice of the reigning status quo and concentration of power in the hands of the elite . . . that's a Roman problem. If Jesus succeeded in creating just such an alternative community—and he clearly did, since the movement grew and flourished—then the question is not *whether* he would be crucified, but why it took the Romans so long to do it.

So, come to the table of Jesus in the first century with all these thoughts in your head and look around the circle and see that those who are touching your bread are contagious, contaminating sinners. They will certainly make you sick. This goes without saying. We accept it as fact. There is a leper on one side of you and a prostitute on the other. A perfect storm. One passes you a broken-off piece of bread. The other dips her hand in a common dish and then offers you a portion from her hand. Your mind says that this is wrong, things are badly out of control. But you take what is offered and over the course of the meal you begin to relax, even tell a few jokes. The food in the middle of the circle slowly disappears, as does the bread. A cup of wine gets passed from lip to lip and you forget your squeamish stomach and take your share. And no one is getting sick. Indeed, a few people across the circle from you are claiming they have been healed. The broken loaf has performed a mystery. How is that possible? In a company of "food fools" where everything should be going wrong, it seems that the

---

2. Crossan presented this idea in his speeches on "God and Empire," presented in Matanzas, Cuba, on February 14, 2009. Indeed, a little over thirty years after Jesus, hidden knives became the terrorist weapon of choice in destabilizing the Judean people of Jerusalem prior to the first Jewish revolt in 68 CE.

opposite is happening. When no one is rejected or turned away, people get better, not worse.

Now, we have to examine the difference between curing a disease and healing an illness.

The Healing Power of Bread

Disease is a physical or psychological disorder. It arrives with disabling symptoms or telltale pains. Some diseases will pass with very little intervention on our part. Others require considerable attention in order to dispel them. Others will kill us no matter how we respond.

Every disease has an attendant illness. Illnesses are the sociological, emotional, and spiritual effects of the disease. If I have a disease, people treat me differently and I see myself in a new light. Some diseases impose isolation: smallpox, for instance. Some diseases engender fear in those who live with us: i.e., leprosy. There are times when the disease makes one feel useless (a stroke) or untouchable (AIDS). All these feelings and reactions stem from the illness. Depending on the disease, some illnesses are very mild, as with the common cold. People simply ask us to keep our distance and cover our mouths when we cough. But some diseases can have very severe attendant illnesses. When AIDs and SARS first appeared on the medical scene, there was widespread paranoia and considerable prejudicial treatment of patients.

All people will suffer disease, and therefore, we will all fall victim to illnesses. It seems apparent that current medical treatment and expertise lie in the curing of disease. Yet for many people, the illness is much more important that the disease itself. We know, even when we won't admit it, that eventually a disease will kill us. We have no hope of escaping that fate. But illnesses, the conditions under which we must suffer the disease, are often the more onerous and frightening: social isolation, personal humiliation, and loss of control. These illnesses we can and could heal, if we only thought more consciously about them.

Here's my story of a modern healing:

About fifteen years ago, I had my appendix taken out, and in those days, I was required to be in hospital for a week. No problem! I was in no pain and I got lots of reading done. In a room with four other patients, it was a study in modern medical practice. The fellow beside me was dying—that seemed obvious to everyone. The disease that plagued him was relentless and cruel. He was in little physical pain, but when they changed his dressings, the room filled with such a stench that everyone who could would leave the room. It was such an odious odor that I am sure the wallpaper would have peeled itself off the wall to escape it. I was stuck in my bed, so I suffered. But my discomfort was nothing compared to the man beside me. When I looked into his eyes, all I could see was deep shame. I knew he felt dirty, untouchable, and lost. His body was betraying him, and while his imminent death was a great fear, the loss of dignity was a much greater weight. He was no longer a man; he was just a bad smell that everyone tried to avoid.

Clearly, there was no cure for this fellow's disease and he knew it. But the illness?

On a Saturday morning when things were quiet, I was surprised to see a pretty young nurse pass my bed with a bowl of water and towel. She pulled the curtains around my neighbor and for an hour she gave him a bath and back rub. There was nothing but flimsy cloth separating us, so I could hear everything. She said very little, a few comforting cliches. He was absolutely silent, but when she finally pulled back the drapes, this guy was healed. There was great smile of deep contentment on his face. He had been touched and comforted by an attractive young woman. He was no longer an outcast or untouchable. Her ministrations had brought him back into the community of "worthy people." His illness was healed, and two hours later he died peacefully. I have no idea if that nurse knew what she had done, but that day I witnessed the miracle of healing. She was an instrument of the force of love, a force that can heal any illness.

If we go back to that circle around the table of Jesus, we can understand the healing power of a common loaf. Sinners were not allowed to recline at dinner with the righteous. If you had been excluded from the table, a place where real people commune and where all the great and important decisions are made, you suffer an illness much like my hospital roommate. Quite naturally, you feel invisible and unworthy. The exclusion from the table speaks volumes of your spiritual virtue. You know yourself to be a problem or curse in God's eyes. What a weight.

Now, imagine being invited to the table of a religious authority. One who is respected and whose fame as a great man of God is spreading throughout the countryside. *He* wants to eat with you. Think of Zacchaeus, the tax collector, who goes to lunch with Jesus (Luke 19: 1–10) or the prostitute who crashes the party at Simon's house (Luke 7:36–50). In both instances, the outcast is taken into the dinner circle and healed. They are no longer untouchable. They can hold their head high, healed.

It is the shared common loaf that works the miracle of healing. The unacceptable are accepted. The lost are found, and those people who saw themselves as dead are brought back to life. When we share bread with one another, there is an implicit message of welcoming each other into a place of shared contentment. Moreover, when you pass the loaf to the leper or eat from the same bread as the prostitute, you say to them that they are not diminished outcasts. We are all now on the same level: all are welcome and all are fed by the God of daily bread.

You can now see how the ministry of Jesus is captured in two simple dimensions of the common loaf. He was known throughout all the land of Judea as one who in shared bread offered (1) radical hospitality and (2) real healing. Wherever he went, the Prayer for daily bread was lived out, and for that moment, the world was transformed into the kingdom of God.

8

An Economic Ideology:
"Forgive us our debts . . ."

Baptists

I LIKE BAPTISTS. For my entire life, I have been hired and paid by the United Church of Canada. Never had a job outside that communion—even in my youth. But I love Baptists.

Let me introduce you to a saintly Baptist who embodies my affection for this denomination. His name is Raul Saurez, and he works in a very marginal neighborhood of Habana called Marianao. He is the pastor of a church and community center named after Martin Luther King, Jr. The ministry began as a mission to create humanity and dignity in a poor *barrio*. As the years passed, it became clear that it was not enough to pass out bread to hungry seniors or hold summer camps for kids. While these charitable acts are essential for Christian witness, there was more that was required.

Visiting groups of North Americans would come to help with the work, and they would ask about communism, the socialist understanding of democracy, and the need for economic growth and individual liberty.

Raul began to offer seminars on economic development, community literacy, and political awareness. He would sponsor exchanges between first- and third-world social workers and political ideologues. The Martin Luther King, Jr. Center is now a national educational institution, one of the three religious bridges that span the distance between first-world communities of faith and those in Cuba.

I recall the first time I met Raul. At that point, he had been elected as a federal member of parliament. In Cuba, this position is voluntary—no salaried politicians. Your workplace is obliged to give you time off (the parliament meets three times a year for at least four or five days). Raul was one of four pastors elected to that assembly.

No sooner had he been elected than the question of capital punishment was raised. There was a motion put forward to abolish it, and he put his name on the list of speakers. It was shaping up to be quite a debate.

Given the restrictive nature of the American blockade and the fact that Cuba is a small, isolated island, there was considerable support in the Cuban parliament for continuing capital punishment. They saw it as both a political necessity and a patriotic symbol. Speaker after speaker rose to denounce any attempt to abolish the state's power to execute wrongdoers. Ringing the chimes on jingoistic sentiments, citing every heinous criminal act of recent memory, pointing fingers at a vague menace beyond control—all of these speakers were greeted with great applause. Then Raul stood to speak and asked the assembled to consider the power of forgiveness. He appealed to them for mercy and to hold out the possibility of grace. He concluded by stating that he was a Christian, and he could no longer grant to his government the power to take life. That was God's prerogative alone. He sat down and the 600-seat assembly was absolutely silent. No one knew what to do. Fidel Castro stood soon after and suggested that it would be good to "listen to our brother Raul." The motion was later defeated, and the state retained the power to inflict the ultimate penalty. But since that debate, the law has never been implemented and people speak of a moratorium on capital punishment.

Raul told this story at the conclusion of our gathering. We were standing in a circle, holding hands, and he invited us to look at one another and ask, "Who else will do God's work, if we don't?"

Hearing his testimony, I have never felt more proud of being a Christian, nor more inspired to live out my vocation, whatever that might be.

Since that initial gathering I have often spoken with Raul, usually in the context of taking groups of Christians to Cuba. There are many basic fact-finding questions that people ask him: how do people buy bread? What about free university education? Can you own anything here? Eventually we get around to politics. Someone asks about the socialist system and then we go down the path of exploring foreign investment and commercial development. Why not allow some measures of capitalism and individual entrepreneurship?

Raul is always patient, but he stops the flow of questions and well intentioned suggestions and makes a very important point:

> You must understand that when we speak positively of bringing capitalism to Cuba, we are thinking of the first-world capitalism in which many people benefit from economic exploitation, a capitalism in which there are minimum standards, union wages and benefits. But that will not be the capitalism that comes to this developing island. It will be third-world capitalism that seeks to exploit peasants, paying meager wages and even lower prices for natural resources. This capitalism will take away much more than it brings.

Then the discussion deepens and we speak of the nature of capitalism as it is manifest in other Latin American countries. What becomes evident is that the economic dependency of the South is a tremendous obstacle to lifting the standard of living of many people. The state's best energy is spent paying off loans it has taken out to participate in the game of first-world, corporate capitalism.

Raul concludes with a Spanish play on words: "*Dios no quiere que la deuda externa sea eterna.*" Translated it says, "God doesn't want external debt to be eternal."

And so, we arrive at the next line in the Prayer: "Forgive us our debts as we have forgiven those who have debts with us."

Read the Book

There's a T-shirt slogan making the rounds in Christian churches. It reads, "Life is Short. Pray hard! Read the Book!" It's a great message and I wish more people would follow it. Especially those who wear this T-shirt as a talisman against what they consider to be the erroneous, liberal interpretation of Scripture.

If we do "read the book," we will discover that the Prayer is not an invitation to seek and receive forgiveness for personal sins. I mentioned above that it is not a heaven-bent list of petitions. It is earth-bound, and one of the basic issues it addresses is human indebtedness: loans are the problem. The word in question is the Greek term for debt and it is used by Matthew in his version of the Prayer: ὀφειλήματα [*ofeilímata*]—"indebtedness." Its classic connotation is monetary. Certainly, the first audience would have heard the phrase as a question of financial obligations. Of course, they did use words connoting economic indebtedness as a reference to personal or spiritual matters. There is nothing wrong with these interpretations. But which is more likely? Will an audience forego the obvious meaning of word to seek out the more esoteric, or will the first and foundational connotation hold their attention?

Remember, we have just asked God to institute again a very concrete reality: daily bread. We see bread having mystical power, but first we see it as something we actually eat. Now follow a tangible object like a loaf of shared bread with "forgive us our debts." What will be the initial reaction? Is it not about financial obligations, rather than spiritual ones? It's only with a bit of reflection and perhaps a number of generations of theological debate that the idea of forgiving debt gets translated as the forgiveness of sins.

There are two further reasons why the economic nature of this petition seems to make sense: one is theological and the second is sociological.

First: theology. The idea of forgiving debts is not original to Jesus. In fact, the Prayer is making a reference to an ancient theological principle called "jubilee economics." Found in Deuteronomy 15 and Leviticus 25, the basic idea is to restrain human greed and to close the gap between the rich and poor. The God of Israel, who gifted the promised land to the people, does not want anyone to fall behind through excessive exploitation. The community of chosen ones is built on the principle that all should enjoy their share of the fruits of creation, and while regular human activity will result in certain "redistributions" which favor a few over many others, these inequalities are not to be interpreted as eternal nor as evidence of any divine sanction. God's justice will not allow it.

To achieve this more egalitarian society, jubilee economics were proclaimed. Following a cycle of seven-year periods, it was proposed that every seventh year, debts between God's people would be written off: those who had been enslaved to pay off debts would be freed, the land was to remain fallow, cattle and farm animals were also to be given a break from the regular routine of labor. Strangers and foreigners were to have special protection in this seventh year so that, in their vulnerability, they were not abused.

Every fiftieth year, land was to be returned to its original owners—there was to be a general redemption. The land was not to be held in perpetuity by a few, it had to go back to its original family.

The jubilee is lived out every week when on the seventh day we all take a rest. Even though Sabbath laws are now observed more in the breach than the observance, they still make it clear that no one can be worked endlessly. Everyone needs a regular break. The principle of an "every six day" rest is found even deeper in Scripture in the first creation story. It's an explanation of how our world is structured. It is based on God's blessing and God's rest.

These jubilee precepts are founded on the simple fact that all we have, all the earth and its fruits, belongs to God. Ownership is a fallacy, and we resort to a spirit of proprietorship far too often as means for personal pretense.

By requiring remission of loans, the people are incorporating their faith in God in a political ideology. The whole point is that our trust and hope in God must be concrete in order for it to be real. There is no purpose in praying for God's justice and yet doing nothing to ensure that it becomes the reigning principle of our daily lives.

So, the Prayer revives an ancient tradition of trust. The people around Jesus were hearkening back to an age of radical faith in God when they said to themselves, "We will be the people who forgive loans. There will be no indebtedness among us, for all that exists, all that anyone has, is first of all a gift of God and so it should be shared with all." They claimed that just and egalitarian space for themselves every time they recited Jesus' Prayer.

Not Crazy, Not Yet

I can feel your eyes glazing over. When I begin to explore the notion of moratoriums of debt and the return of real estate, the modern mind goes numb. We can't get our heads around the principles of jubilee economics—they seem far too utopian and impractical.

May I make a confession? I have invited you into this exploration of the Prayer because I have seen examples of the jubilee lived out in a very concrete place. I chose to write this book in Cuba because there is a very different understanding of land tenure here. In Cuba, no one is allowed to be an "owner" in the traditional sense. People have homes, enjoy the rights and responsibilities of proprietorship, but they are more like permanent stewards. Cubans have the right of dwelling in a house, and they have the responsibility to care for, decorate, and maintain it. But you don't own it . . . not in the traditional sense. Some Cubans say they only own the roof. That is to say you have the right to build on your roof whatever you like and treat it like your property. And many do just that. However, there is no serious speculation in real estate because you cannot build up equity by owning several houses and renting them out to others. No one owns apartment complexes or hotels. Each person can only own three pieces of real estate: a city dwelling, a beach house, and a farm. No more. Of course, there are always "complications" that allow for human greed to rear its ugly head. People can "exchange" their home for another, legally. There are monetary incentives that may make this exchanging a source of income. Likewise, there are people who "occupy" more than one apartment because the death of a loved one has given them the right to dwell in a separate apartment or house. It's not perfect and there is no one who is truly satisfied. With the introduction of some versions of a market economy, this situation is shifting. Private B&Bs are popping up all over.

Since there is an unspoken "right" to an occupied dwelling and yet there are not enough to go around, housing remains a huge problem in Cuba. People live in overcrowded homes and the fact that multiple generations must live in the same dwelling makes privacy a scarce commodity. The endless tangle of family dynamics would leave most northerners breathless. There's a joke that says that in the marriage service, the line about "till death do us part" should be changed to "till in-laws do us part."

And yet, the principles of house tenure or stewardship remain unchanged and serve the general purpose behind jubilee economics. No one is able to leap ahead of others through excessive and personal exploitation of the land. In spite of very clear problems, the basic principle holds true. As we restrain avarice and flatten the levels of inequality within our society, we achieve something close to justice.

The second reason, that I would argue that this petition about "forgiving debts" is first and foremost about a financial transaction and not a spiritual contract, is the sociological framework of first-century Palestine. In just over a hundred years, the people of Israel revolted three times, once just before the start of the common era, once in 68 CE, and again in 130 CE. Their land would be occupied for well over 500 years, but all the resistance happens in this relatively condensed period of time. What focused the people's animosity?

There are certainly many factors which led to an overt act of revolt against an occupying force, but clearly under the specific particularities I outlined above, I suspect there was a groundswell of anger surrounding what was happening to the land. Something unacceptable was changing the people's use or tenure of God's sacred trust.

Put together three bits of historical/archaeological evidence, and we see a pattern emerge. First, in the years surrounding the ministry of Jesus, archeologists tell us that the boundary stones of farm plots were moving. Small farms were squeezed and larger lands were joined together. It looks very much like the depopulation of the land, as larger estates were consolidated. Second, we know that in this same period, a very large portion of the land was held in the hands of a few families. In fact, in lower Galilee over 50 percent of the land was owned by only three family clans. Finally, taxes were rising. The building projects of Herod the Great and his son, Antipas, were sucking up more resources from the bottom levels of the populace. The accumulative result of these factors was the loss of the land.

As Roman occupation was strengthened through the bolstering and enriching of local elites through increased commercialization, the sacred trust of the land was betrayed. It seems obvious that small families were losing their farms to wealthy elites who favored monoculture and increased yields for export rather than local consumption. There is no need to resort to an explanation of excessive force or outright seizure to explain how the loss of land takes place. You lose your land all too easily. Let's say you are a farmer with a few hectares of good land in the valley below Nazareth. Your farm supports your extended family: a few acres of cultivated grains, mostly barley. There are the domestic animals: chickens, a couple of goats, and an ewe who can no longer produce offspring. You have a few sheep in a herd that is pastured up on the mountains. A household garden supplies a few vegetables in season, and you are fortunate enough to have an olive tree for shade, fruit, and oil. Everything is well, until a surprisingly poor harvest squeezes your resources. Usually, you'd borrow from or barter with a neighbor, but everyone is in the same predicament. So, you go to your patron, the town aristocrat, and you pledge your sheep against the needed grain for planting next year's crop. There is no interest on the loan, for that is unrighteous among Judeans. If you default on the loan and are unable to repay the grain, then the sheep goes to the overlord. You can see a pattern, can't you? If a few years of drought are matched by an untimely demise of farm animals, the prospects get desperate. Eventually, the land is pledged and lost as peasant farmers find themselves caught with mounting needs, crushing taxes, and diminishing resources.

As you leave the land that was once held as a family trust, a gift of God to your parents and grandparents, you are burdened with shame and resentment. You feel humiliated for having lost the family's fortunes. It is not your fault, but you still feel the sting of your personal failure. The loss of the land goes hand in hand with your loss of well-being. The relative security of farm food is snatched away. You can no longer see past the next day's pay. You will now have to live with relatives, in a more diminished lodging, for certain. Every morning you will rise and go to the marketplace, hoping to get a day's worth of work and a silver coin to buy food to feed your dependents.

As you wait in the marketplace, you meet with others like yourself and you begin to exchange stories. There is a growing awareness that the loss of the family farm is more widespread than you imagined. Lots of people have been caught in the cycle of debt and foreclosure. As you tell jokes about the landlords, you all begin to sneer and swear about the state of the nation. You can't put your finger on it, but you know something wrong is afoot. Things aren't the way they used to be and it irks you to see what appears to be a trend to treat the land like a commodity to be endlessly exploited. "It's just not right," you all mutter as you walk off to another twelve hours of working the land that once belonged to you and your neighbors. Can we not see that covert resistance and overt revolt are understandable, if not inevitable?

Bread for Today, No Debt for Tomorrow

It's all about money and land. One can hardly see this petition as anything other than a way to focus on the crisis that faced the people around Jesus.

Ever wonder why Jesus is always down at the seashore? Aren't there towns and villages up in the hills? Why does the story keep coming back to the lake? Here's a suggestion: Reading between the lines, it would not be an exaggeration to suggest that Jesus' ministry around the Sea of Galilee was motivated by the fact that what had been happening on the land was now being transplanted to the fishing community. Once fishing had been free, but as taxes and licenses were imposed, the flash point of resistance became the anger and resentment of fishers who were losing control over their heritage and trade.

In the context of these two factors: the theological tradition of showing trust in God by living by a seven-year cycle of writing off debt and the sociological phenomenon of the loss of land through debt and foreclosure, it seems entirely appropriate to see this petition as a very concrete expression of financial forgiveness. The people of Jesus were clear. They want to live by the ancient rules of jubilee.

Take the Prayer at its face value and you have an astounding political program. Put the petition about bread and this one about debts together, and we might capture the sense of the kingdom of God in this fashion: the people gather and claim a space in God's justice, saying, "Let us be the people who live by today's bread and who suffer no debt tomorrow."

Let us imagine the people of this kingdom of God. How would they appear? They are gathered at the end of a tough day. Some laborers have found work, others waited all day with no hope. Some fishers caught a couple of fish, others had no luck. There are three prostitutes who come with renewed pride and loaves of bread. A couple of lepers who live on the edge of the village have brought some root vegetables. There are kids playing among the adults. They have brought the gift of their laughter. Now we form our circle and recline in our places. Everything we have is in the middle, and it is indeed a feast. Those of us who had nothing to offer feel no shame. We'll get our chance to provide for others, who today were fortunate, but who may not be blessed with food tomorrow. Looking at the bountiful meal in the middle of our circle, you can hardly miss the sense of abundance. God has blessed us again with the miracle of his kingdom. We pass one of the loaves around, so that everyone shares a piece of bread before the meal starts. We know to whom we belong and in whose realm we live.

A Good Imitation

In the shared loaf, both of these proclamations about bread and debt become real and reassuring for the people of God's kingdom. There is no doubt. Of course, we won't make any distinctions between our physical and spiritual sense of contentedness and reassurance. We just know that, in the company of Jesus, we have come home.

Now, I want to tell you about what just happened. I don't usually speak of God's intervention, but it is difficult not to see apparent coincidences as a bit more than random.

It has been my good fortune to be given time to write this book by a Presbyterian church in Habana, Cuba. I came for a month to preach, teach, and make bread. Before I left the North, I received a message stating that the church was in trouble. They had a program of feeding lunch to seniors, but the sewer pipes passing under the kitchen had broken, polluting the water supply. The lunch program for twenty-five elders had to be suspended. So, they asked if I could come and make bread, feed them somehow.

I filled my suitcase with yeast, mixing bowls, and bread flour—at least enough to get started. After a quick consultation, it made the most sense not to make lunch. Rather, if I rose early in the morning, I could make bread for breakfast, which was the traditional Cuban diet for early morning: coffee, warm milk, and bread. Couldn't ask for better.

My days have been shaped by writing and bread-making. I rise at 4:20 AM and mix the dough. At 6:00, it's punched down, shaped into buns, and baked by 8:30. The seniors start to appear with containers for heated milk and bags for bread. Over the weeks, the numbers have been rising. Word is spreading that fresh bread is available at the church for free.

Mid-morning, I leave the distribution of bread to seniors to my Cuban colleagues and head to my bedroom to write. However, there is no stopping people's love of bread. Bible studies are now anticipated with particular eagerness because I make bread to share. The church leaders have been asking if I could make pizza for the beginning of their meetings. Bread has the blessed quality of inspiring enthusiasm and fun.

So, here's what just happened: I have been writing these lines about the forgiveness of debt and the way in which shared bread communicates the assurance of God's acceptance. I went out into the sunshine to fill up my coffee cup. Cuban coffee, which is really a form of espresso coffee, is certainly the best I have ever tasted, and while I don't wait around very long in the morning as the bread is being given out, I wouldn't miss my share of the morning coffee and milk. As I am walking back across the church square, Louis stops me to talk.

He is the church bus driver, but so much more. He is a diminutive elder who has a well-chewed cigar held between his fingers at all times and a mischievous smile fixed permanently on his lips. A man of many talents, I have watched him change the broken clutch on the church bus in the middle of a deserted stretch of highway . . . with nothing more than hand tools. He recites the poetry of Jose Marti, the national hero, and sings his best-known song, "Guantanamara" with a rich, clear tenor voice.

Today, he stopped me on my way back to my room. He wanted to impart a small reflection. He loves to tell a story and even more to embellish it with poetic references. So, Louis began by making allusions to a time, 2,000 years ago, when a man was known for bringing people together with bread. "How the multitudes praised it as the stuff of life!" Then, with a twinkle in his eyes, he said that now, in these past few weeks, with so much bread passing from hand, the magic of Jesus' bread is happening again. "It may not be God's kingdom," he whispered, "but it's a good imitation!"

I rest my case: bread in the hands of the faithful turns the ordinary into the extraordinary. "Thy kingdom come!"

9

The Theology of the Kingdom of God: "Thine is the power"

The First Ethic: Table Manners

THE ROOM WAS IN constant shadow. A single lightbulb hanging from the ceiling by its own wiring was waving in the wind that blew through the rock walls. The light would blink on and off. During the moments it flashed on, I could see mats and beds strewn about the floor. Around the walls were blankets rolled up beside straw. In the center of the room right below the light was a large master bed.

I had the sinking feeling that I was being shown my bedroom. Eight hours of walking straight up into the Himalayas, close enough to see Everest in the morning and this was the "hotel"? Our guide had kept us going through the arduous day long trek by saying that we would rest well in the "hotel" at the top of the pass.

This is our rest!?

Clearly, our host was showing us his best room. In fact, it was so good he was going to sleep here too, along with his many children and their progeny.

Fatigue stilled my tongue, and I took a blanket as far from the main bed as I could get, hoping to sleep before anyone decided to get amorous. The room was directly above the kitchen where the fires still burned, and since there was no chimney, the wood beneath my blanket reeked of soot and grease. Centuries of cook-smoke had baked the floorboards.

All the while, I was smiling, bowing, nodding, hoping that I was not trespassing any unnoticeable rule of etiquette. That was the worst side of that night. I was paralyzed by an anxiety that I might prove myself ungrateful or unconsciously insult my very generous host. He was so obviously trying to honor his guests with his best offering.

It was then that I realized that the first and foundational ethic of human existence is politeness.

Without common household courtesies and table etiquette, our world would be a wasteland of chaos and immorality. I mean that. This is not a trick.

When we teach our children to say "please" and "thank you," or to not chew their food with their mouths open, we train them in the primary lesson of ethics. At meal time, they learn the concrete difference between "could" and "should."

Of course, politeness is an empty ethic in the sense that it is culturally conditioned. There is no eternal moral commandment that forms the basis for politeness. What is acceptable in one society is a scandal in another. Hence arises many a cross-cultural misunderstanding. For instance, in the above mentioned "hotel" it would be the height of rudeness to refuse to sleep with our host in his bedroom. We could have been left on the "porch" to fend for ourselves, but this man was rolling out the red carpet by showing us to his master suite. In moments like that night, the need for propriety is indisputable. Besides weathering international encounters, on a deeper level, learning the lesson of politeness, we discover the benefits of restricting our personal behavior. We exercise moral restraint and begin to understand that not all that can be done, should be done.

How often, as an ethicist, do people ask me about the reasons behind evil behavior? "Why do people do bad things?" My first answer is always, "Because they can." Bad people are not born, they grow into their evil ways because they have not been taught and trained in the need to control personal power. Just because you can do something is not permission to do it.

In its foundation, etiquette is about shaping and restraining power, and from this place we build a better world.

Would you mind coming back with me to the first-century dinner table? There is one more lesson to learn—this time we will explore the nature of the kingdom—how the Prayer concludes with "thine is the power and the glory." What exactly is God's power and how does it function?

I suppose I should begin by explaining the way things actually looked in a dining room in the time of Jesus. First, forget Leonardo da Vinci and his painting of the Last Supper. It never happened that way—ever. The Mediterranean world had tables and chairs, but they were never used for eating. No one would think of pulling a chair up to the table to enjoy a meal. In our day and age, you could eat your dinner sitting on the hood of a car. It would work, but why would you do it? In the first century, there were plenty of flat surfaces, but to eat in that world was to recline on your left elbow and lie in either a circle or an open U shape. Head and right hand closer to the center, feet to the outside.

In wealthy Roman circles, there were reclining beds or what we would recognize as a settee. But in the peasant world of Jesus, it was the floor or nothing. There might be a rug, but more than likely you would lie down on the hard-beaten floor of the host's home.

The food would be delivered on a common platter, into the center of reclining guests. As I mentioned above, there were no discrete portions. No personal utensils. You ate with your right hand, dipping it into food that was shared by all. There might be bread to act as a scoop or temporary plate, but it would be impolite to take food off the central platter to put it on some bread at your own place. Comparable in our world to taking the common pitcher of water and setting it beside your cup, as if it was only for your individual use.

Given that we are going to be sticking our fingers in each other's dinner, you can imagine that cleanliness was more than a common courtesy. It was essentially a responsible, necessary act.

Hosts were required, by the rules of hospitality, to offer each guest the opportunity to clean their hands. Feet were routinely washed as an act of welcoming and, to put it bluntly, as a means of reducing the level of both contagion and odor. Oh yes, another small point: don't mention your feet. They are the lowly part of the body and in polite company we don't use four-letter words or speak of our feet (which is essentially the same thing).

All of this etiquette reigned over formal dinners. I can imagine families huddling around a common pot set down on the dried mud of a courtyard or in the shade of a tree. But in a formal setting, there were clear expectations on everyone's part. We have to realize that the banquet was one of the key mechanisms for keeping and enhancing honor. We all take part in the ritual because we all enjoy the benefits of the enhanced honor, our host, and by extension his worth as our patron. The host was required to offer food and hospitality in extravagant portions. As guests, we are bound by propriety to be equally profuse in our praise and gratitude. No superlative on either side is wasted.

It is easy to see this show of hosting/eating as a charade. Imagine a black-tie dinner in a high-class country club. All the niceties of table manners are essential aspects of reinforcing the status quo. Moreover, aesthetically, it is a pleasing aspect of the dinner ritual for people to follow carefully prescribed roles. On the more profound emotional level, following table manners gives us a sense of security. Everything is right with the world.

Let's follow a story of a special dinner described in the Gospel of Luke (7:36–50). We will discover the nature of divine power found in this kingdom of God, which we invoke in the Prayer. It is perhaps the most discomforting piece of Christian Scripture we possess. I would suggest you read it slowly with as few "Christian" assumptions as possible. Look at it as a story about a dinner meeting and apply the standards of etiquette required by that time:

36 One of the Pharisees invited him for dinner, he entered the Pharisee's house and reclined at the table.

37 A local woman, who was a sinner, found out that he was having dinner at the Pharisee's house. She suddenly showed up with an alabaster jar of myrrh.

38 . . . and stood there behind him weeping at his feet. Her tears wet his feet, and she wiped them dry with her hair, she kissed his feet and anointed them with the myrrh.

39 The Pharisee who had invited him saw this and said to himself, "If this man were a prophet, he would know who this is and what kind of woman is touching him, since she is a sinner."

40 And Jesus answered him, "Simon I have something to tell you." "Teacher," he said, "Speak up."

41 "This money lender had two debtors, one owed five hundred silver coins and the other fifty.

42 Since neither could pay, he wrote off both debts. Now which of them will love him more?"

43 Simon answered, "I would imagine, the one for whom he wrote off the larger debt." And he said to him, "You're right."

44 Then turning to the woman, he said to Simon, "Do you see this woman? I walked into your house and you didn't offer me water for my feet, yet she has washed my feet with her tears and dried them with her hair.

45 You didn't offer me a kiss, but she hasn't stopped kissing my feet since I arrived.

46 You didn't anoint my head with oil, but she has anointed my feet with myrrh.

47 For this reason, I tell you, her sins, many as they are, have been forgiven as this outpouring of her love shows. But the one who is forgiven little shows little love."

48 And he said to her, "Your sins have been forgiven."

49 But those having dinner with him began to mutter to themselves, "Who is this who even forgives sins?"

50 And he said to the woman, "Your trust has saved you, go in peace."[1]

If you need to read the passage again, go right ahead. We're going to undertake a close reading of this text, a Bible study if you will. So, have your questions ready and we'll see if I can answer them as we go along. I will walk through the story, verse by verse, offering commentary and some historical background. When we are finished, we will ask ourselves two things: What is the portrait of Jesus that this story inspires and why does Luke portray Jesus in this manner?

36 One of the Pharisees invited him for dinner, he entered the Pharisee's house and reclined at the table.

Let us begin by getting in our mind all of the expectations and etiquette I described above as they pertain to this specific story. We've been invited to dinner and that means we have a responsibility to honor our host, for in that act rests our own worth as well. We want to be generous in our praise to the host.

Luke borrows this story from Mark, who uses it as a foreshowing of Jesus' crucifixion. In Mark's gospel, the anointing of Jesus happens two days before his crucifixion, and the unnamed woman who pours oil on Jesus is acting out an allusion to the anointing of dead bodies. It's like she is performing the required ablutions before he is executed. In this story, there is also Mark's affirmation of Jesus' messiahship. In Hebrew, the word "messiah" means just that: the anointed one, and in Greek it is "Christ." As if using sign language, this unknown woman acts out the clear message that this Jesus of Nazareth is also the "messiah," or the "anointed one," or the "Christ." A dramatic affirmation.

---

1. This is the translation take from the Scholars version, as noted above.

Mark sets this prophetic story in the house of Simon the Leper. So, we have a marvelous picture of the new King of the people of God being chosen, anointed, and empowered in the lowest possible social context. There is no throne room or palace for this "king." Let Pilate and Herod hog the limelight of status and wealth. God's chosen one comes from a different place altogether. His coronation takes place in what is essentially a crack house.

Luke adopts the story, but switches the two chief factors of Mark's story: Simon becomes a Pharisee, the other end of the righteousness scale from that of a leper—we have just moved the dinner from a back-alley dumpster hovel to the white-table banquet hall—and the drama happens separate from any allusion to the cross. There is no attempt to make a connection between the act of anointing and the coming messiahship of Jesus. In Luke's hands, the oil will be a tool for hospitality and delight.

Now, imagine someone telling a well-known story. What does it mean when they alter certain key details? Some embellishment is allowed, but when we change the context and central allusion of a story, we're going beyond the convention of poetic license. I get suspicious. In my mind, this level of change usually signals a difference of opinion. Either the original story contained mistakes, was not clear enough about some essential aspect, or the storyteller wants to make an entirely different point than has been hitherto expressed. This is not poor plagiarism or unthinking excessiveness. Luke is going to make a point in contradistinction to Mark.

> 37 A local woman, who was a sinner, found out that he was having dinner at the Pharisee's house. She suddenly showed up with an alabaster jar of myrrh.

Watch the words. The woman comes in "suddenly." It's as if she bursts into the circle when no one is expecting her. There was no prior notice. She's a party crasher, an uninvited guest.

What's more, she's a sinner—Luke tells us that up front. Mark leaves it to the audience's imagination. But Luke wants to be precise, so, using the euphemism of his day, he is saying, "We have a prostitute here, folks!" The alabaster jar of myrrh is further evidence, in case you didn't catch Luke's point. Prostitutes hung a jar of anointment around their necks as both advertisement and enticement. It was like a red light, or a calling card: 1-800-Call-Babe.

Moreover, she's an unwelcome sinner in a Pharisee's house. Oh, this is marvelously uncomfortable. We have oil and water: the contaminating and impolite hooker breaking into the carefully orchestrated propriety of a very pure circle of men sharing a formal dinner.

Picture a presidential dinner. Everyone is seated around the table, dinner places arranged perfectly, wine goblets and silver cutlery everywhere, black ties all round and enough etiquette to choke a horse. In walks a whore from the street with black boots reaching up to her hips, a tight, neon pink tank top, a leather whip over one shoulder, and a leather vest falling from the other. She sashays across the room and slinks up to the guest of honour and says in a sultry alto voice, "Hi, honey!"

Feel uncomfortable yet? Just wait. It gets worse:

> 38 . . . and stood there behind him weeping at his feet. Her tears wet his feet, and she wiped them dry with her hair, she kissed his feet and anointed them with the myrrh.

Right. I am not sure I should be watching this. Do we have a bit of home hospitality going on or is this more like the foreplay to a seriously intimate act? Is this prostitute hitting on Jesus or just being nice? Either way, the actions described by Luke are certainly excessive. The feet were such an undesirable part of the body that slaves would use run-off water to wash them and a second-rate towel to dry them. This woman is much more personal. She uses what she has brought with her—tears and hair—to perform this. Washing feet was the usual responsibility of the host. In many cases, a necessary act to reduce odors and contagions in the dining room. It goes without saying that the host would not perform this menial task himself. That was given to the lowest strata of the family: female servants or slaves. So, the actions of the woman are not exceptional, but using her tears and hair to perform it presumes serious intimacy and is both touching and very sensual.

I would be surprised if Luke wants the audience to see this action as suggestive of sexual intercourse. Nevertheless, let's allow Jesus to be fully human. He must have enjoyed the attention and the pleasure of being ministered to in such a personal manner. For the little Puritan voice in each one of us that expects Jesus to float above sensual delights of the flesh, let's recognize that he doesn't tell her to stop, nor does he interrupt her ministrations even while he tells the parable to Simon. This is an act of delight that others are witnessing, and Jesus likes it!

Have you ever asked what it means when the woman breaks the alabaster jar? Without knowing about how this vessel functions, we would simply pass over the gesture as a necessary part of getting the oil out of its container. But if the alabaster jar is a "tool of the trade," then breaking it signals two possible facts. Either the prostitute is quitting the trade or she is lavishing an essential and expensive occupational instrument on only one client—a gesture of very serious affection and affiliation! It's like she has just used up a year's worth of her salary servicing one client.[2] Has she been with Jesus before and is now paying him back for a previous gesture of love or healing with "all that she has"? Wait and see!

> 39 The Pharisee who had invited him saw this and said to himself, "If this man were a prophet, he would know who this is and what kind of woman is touching him, since she is a sinner."

Simon wakes up. I can picture him doing a double-take as he drags his eyes away from this woman's sensuality. He recovers from the shock, and Luke takes us into his head to read his apprehensions firsthand. The Pharisee starts to question if he did the right thing by inviting Jesus to dinner. A note on Pharisees: they were *not* the bad people we make them out to be. We suffer from a bit of first-century invective when we describe them as mean-spirited, narrow-minded gatekeepers. In the seventies and eighties of the common era, Christians and Pharisees were fighting with each other over who would take over Judaism when the temple fell, and so each side had its share of name-calling and muckraking. Christians portrayed their competitors, the Pharisees, as hopelessly anal retentive. But the truth is, they were the great innovators of their day. A lay movement, the Pharisees proposed that believers did not have to go to the temple to be righteous, one could be pure in heart. They enjoyed debate and respected spiritual authority.

Simon invited Jesus to dinner because he wanted to engage this man in theological debate. There may have been some tension, but it was not necessary to have Jesus to dinner if all you wanted to do was attack his position. And as the conclusion of the parable suggests, Simon respects Jesus as a great "teacher." Let us not paint Simon as a conniving patriarch. He was simply doing "the right thing" by having this famous rabbi to dinner.

Now he is wondering if Jesus is living up to his reputation. Surely, he would know what kind of woman is touching him. She is defiling the house in general and Jesus in particular. Any spiritual guru worth his salt

---

2. In Mark's gospel (Mark 14:5) we are told the special ointment is valued at over three hundred silver coins, which is code for a year's salary since the average laborer's wage is one coin per day.

would know this and pull away from her in order to preserve his personal righteousness. It's only common sense.

> 40 And Jesus answered him, "Simon, I have something to tell you."
> "Teacher," he said, "Speak up."

Jesus is exactly what Simon thinks. He is a surprising religious leader for he can read another's thoughts. If Luke were writing a TV drama, he might have the voice-over narrator say something like: "He is not as stupid as he looks." Rather than let things unravel without comment, Jesus invites Simon into a debate, and, as I mentioned, Simon responds with a very reverent response calling Jesus by "teacher." It would be like the university lecturer saying to an invited guest, "Tell me what you think, professor." Very professional and polite.

> 41 "This money lender had two debtors, one owed five hundred silver coins and the other fifty.

We're back to debts. Obviously, the problem of indebtedness is commonplace. People will understand the stresses and strains of debt without having to be told. A good storyteller's technique: use the "hot topic" of the social context which people already know—Jesus is clearly a master storyteller! The amounts owed are substantial. The first person has a debt equal to one and a half year's wages. The second owes a bit more than a month's wages.

> 42 Since neither could pay, he wrote off both debts. Now which of them will love him more?"
> 43 Simon answered, "I would imagine, the one for whom he wrote off the larger debt." And he said to him, "You're right."

Do we see a pattern here? We're in the world of the previous chapter of this book, in which debts are forgiven. Maybe the money lender is a righteous man fulfilling his sabbatical duty. Perhaps he is just being merciful. Either way, it's a surprising twist to the parable. I can imagine the first audience heaving a sigh of relief or gasping in wonder at the turns of events.

Now the big question! How do we gauge love? Is there a reciprocal relationship between the amount of love we show and the measure of forgiveness we have been offered? I don't see this as a trick question. Jesus is simply asking the obvious. There can be no other response than the one Simon gives. Those who are forgiven much will love in proportion to their debt.

Can I stop the action? Picture the woman who is still wiping Jesus' feet, and Simon who is letter-perfect in his treatment of Jesus. At this stage, what connections would Jesus be trying to make? The understandable one is to see the woman as the great debtor who owes much and Simon as the one who owes little. There seems little question that Simon sees it that way. He's not a sinner, she is!

But can we leave room for Jesus' sense of irony? Could it be that he is actually implying that the one who owes much is Simon, someone who is unaware of how much he actually owes because he has presumed himself to be debt-free? Hear Jesus saying with an ironic smile, "Oh, no. Simon, this is not a story for people like you who are *so righteous*, but the one at my feet who really needs to hear it." In that case, the parable could be seen not as a bit of scolding, but rather as a half-joking invitation for Simon to drop the pretense and get serious about his own spiritual poverty.

Back to the main stage. Things are about to get nasty. Hang on to to your polite cliches, Jesus is about to break all the boundaries.

> 44 Then turning to the woman, he said to Simon, "Do you see this woman? I walked into your house and you didn't offer me water for my feet, yet she has washed my feet with her tears and dried them with her hair.
>
> 45 You didn't offer me a kiss, but she hasn't stopped kissing my feet since I arrived.
>
> 46 You didn't anoint my head with oil, but she has anointed my feet with myrrh.

In these three verses, the serenely polite Sunday School Jesus disappears, and in his place, we have a social lout. I can hardly read this tirade without squirming. Jesus not only insults his host three times, he uses foul language and vulgar expressions to do it.

In our world, it would be gauche and insulting to question a host's motives and attentiveness. Imagine if you invited me for dinner, and I interrupted the conversation to comment on the poor quality of the main course! What would you think if I told you I thought the ambiance of the dining room was substandard? How about I pick up a fork and read the imprint in the silver and laugh about how it's not real, just plate?

You'd be furious, embarrassed, and humiliated.

Now translate those feelings to Simon and add a hundredfold emphasis. In the Mediterranean world, even today, you do not question a host's motives, not to his face, and rarely even in private.

Can you imagine Simon's chagrin? Jesus is listing off all the faults of his hospitality in front of the other guests and this woman. Did he tick them off on upheld fingers? Humiliation is hanging in the air as thick as smoke! Simon didn't wash, kiss, or comfort at all. Not like this *woman*.

Oh, yes. These verses start with a very interesting invitation for everyone to look at the woman. I can imagine everyone up to that point was trying very hard *not* to see her. Averted eyes, collective interest in staring at the ceiling, what did they do? Somehow, they all tried to avoid acknowledging her presence.

But Jesus calls all eyes to her, "Do you see this woman?" Obviously, they all did, so the question is really more of an affirmation of the legitimacy of her presence. She's not a nobody and you can't wish her away. What did this say about Luke's understanding of the Jesus movement?

"And the four-letter words?" you ask. Yes . . . those.

To add insult to the great injury Jesus has just inflicted, he says "feet" no less than four times. It would be like Jesus preaching in a prim and proper church and complaining to the congregation: "I came into the church and no one washed my crotch! What's the matter with you people?" Vulgar and excessive.

If you're not asking yet about Luke's sanity, you should be. What is he trying to do? He takes a story from Mark, in which Jesus is a noble sacrificial monarch, and turns him into an abusive bully and boor. Why? Let's leave that question hanging for a moment.

> 47 For this reason, I tell you, her sins, many as they are, have been forgiven as this outpouring of her love shows. But the one who is forgiven little shows little love."

Jesus makes his point in this verse. The woman's ministrations are not an attempt to receive a benediction from Jesus. She's not giving in the hope of getting something in return—she has received her reward. This outpouring of affection is evidence of how much she has already been given. An essential point in the science of theology. The formula is: God gives grace and love freely, extravagantly. We respond by loving in our turn. Christians who hold out the carrot of God's forgiveness, if only people will repent of sins and "accept Jesus as Savior and Lord," have the equation backwards. God's love *is*. Period. It is always present and flowing toward us. There is no condition, behavior, or magic recitation that will turn on the tap, so to speak. There is no sacrifice required. You don't have to go to the temple or pay your tithes. Righteousness is not about earning our merit. God loves us already. Nothing we do, or don't do, will change that.

And those who recognize and receive this love of God know they have had their debts written off and quite genuinely want to respond by loving others with the same extravagance.

48 And he said to her, "Your sins have been forgiven."

In keeping with what has just been said about the forgiveness of sins being an act of God that has already taken place, I read this verse as a statement of fact and not as the granting of forgiveness. Jesus is telling the woman that she got it right.

49 But those having dinner with him began to mutter to them-selves, "Who is this who even forgives sins?"

And like human life everywhere, no good deed goes unpunished. The gossip gallery has more grist for their mill. Like so many before and after them, these guests will complain about Jesus, his eating habits, and etiquette. They misunderstand Jesus' words and see his conversation with the woman as an unusual and presumptuous affront. "He's opened up our dinner tables to riffraff and he thinks he's got special power?" That's their complaint.

50 And he said to the woman, "Your trust has saved you, go in peace."

The story concludes with a reaffirmation that the woman has been saved, and not by the intervention of Jesus, but by her own trust. It's not his words or her actions that have brought about salvation. God has done that already. It is her trust in the justice of God and God's desire to offer her love that has restored her. She enjoys God's peace because she has faith.

The Key Question

So again, what is Luke's point? I believe we can see that he changes the story significantly in order to portray Jesus in a very peculiar light. What is his point? Does he seriously see Jesus as a buffoon who doesn't know the basics of table manners? Are we following a social rebel who doesn't care about protecting people's sense of order and well-being? I believe Luke shapes this story in order to push the believer to a choice. It's like a testimonial that ends with the finger pointed directly at the audience. "What about you?" Either this Jesus fellow is an oaf that can't keep his mouth shut, or he is an anointed messiah who has come to change everything—right down to table manners.

How do you choose?

Luke wants us to see Jesus as the one who has come to turn the world upside down. He's born in a barn, he cavorts with the down-and-out people of the world because he wants to show us that God has no regard for human societal standards. In God's reign, the relationships are all different. Power is not used to "lord over" the vulnerable and to control the weak. So, he uses this story to push us all to the brink. Will you follow Simon and his carefully constructed world of propriety that keeps sinners in their place or will you join Jesus in changing everything: lifting up the lowly and celebrating God's extravagant love?

That's your choice. Luke is waiting.

A New Understanding of Power

While we contemplate how we'll answer Luke, let's dig a little deeper. This story points to a rethinking of the nature of human power; the capacity to get things done is shifting. In the company of God's reign, it is not a top-down affair. The pyramid of power represented by the Pharisees and religious authorities is a replication of imperial structures: power in that world is exercised by a few on behalf of many. To achieve any result, you work the pyramid. In the kingdom of God, we have something much closer to a circle; through sharing we achieve a new community.

In the time of Jesus, the power was exercised through force, often violent. Nations and peoples who opposed the imperial ambitions were subjugated to imperial rule, and once they swallowed their pride and accepted their place in the food chain, peace was declared. That's what we call the *Pax Romana.* Throughout the Roman world, there are temples and monuments which celebrate this power of empire. Put simply: we get peace through violence and war.[3] In contrast, the power of God we celebrate in the Lord's Prayer is a power that arises when all are welcome and given

---

3. For greater detail on the exact location and nature of these monuments to Roman peace, see Crossan, *God and Empire,* 19–21.

their rightful place. The reign of God appears when Luke's story is lived out: the lost and untouchables are welcomed into the circle. Real peace arises from God's justice. In the company of Jesus, we have a new order being established and it will influence everything.

A final note on the justice of God. There are two kinds of justice: retributive and distributive. The former is about punishment for the evil-doers, and the latter is about the just distribution of God's blessings. We sometimes confuse the two, or assume that God's justice is only about de-livering judgement. In its worst form, we assign the God of punishment to the Hebrew Scriptures, and the loving distributive God to the Christian Scriptures. While this may be a very satisfying analysis for Christians, it is false. From the beginning to the end of the Bible, the message is consistent: God blesses this earth with bounty and desires all to enjoy it.

Getting Our Story Straight

The Prayer concludes with an affirmation that all is in God's hands. As if setting the record straight, it invites those who pray to remember the proper order of things. It's like an invitation to keep your eyes on the ball. So, let's conclude with a recapitulation of our story.

There are many reasons to dismiss the Internet as a very expensive toy, a growing modern distraction. But I doubt if anyone would argue against the usefulness of Google Earth—the program that offers you the ability to plot your travels in advance. Prior to the Internet, we were restricted to fold-out maps and firsthand accounts—maybe a pocket guidebook, if we were lucky. Now, if you want to know where you are headed, you are just a few clicks away from zooming in on your destination. You can even focus on the color of the front door you hope will open for you. We click our way closer and closer to our final destination and then, hoping to see a bit more to the left or right, we focus the satellite image just a tad off center and then lose ourselves in detail. We are so close that we cannot find our way back. The camera lens pans past random trees, bits of sidewalk, unnamed build-ings. There's no signal to help us get our bearings. So, we have to back out again, get a wide-angle view, so to speak, and recover our sense of direction.

That's where we are in our study of this final affirmation of the Prayer. What is the broader picture of God's kingdom and the use of God's power? What are we praising when we say in the Prayer, "Thine is the kingdom and the power and the Glory . . ."? What is the big picture painted by the Bible?

Often in worship, the sermon is like Google Earth at its maximum strength—we drive down to the closest, smallest locations on the map we call Scripture. Dealing with a single word or phrase, a small story or single parable, we are focused on mere drops in the expansive oceans we call the Bible. What would we see if we pulled our focus back? Zoom out?

In a Prius that I test-drove a few years back, there was a voice-activated map program that you could get to work by saying, "Zoom out." When my son, Griffin, came with me, I showed it to him and he immediately shouted, "Zoom out!" Nothing happened. From the backseat, he barked more sternly, "Zoom out." A long pause . . . and then the car replied, "I am sorry, we don't speak Italian." Grif thought it was hilarious. "Dad, the car thinks I'm speaking Italian."

Italian notwithstanding, what would we say if we could ask the Bible to zoom out? Rather than focusing on the single cobblestones that make up our pilgrimage path, what would we see if we backed off to see the whole road, stretching from beginning to end?

Think of the biblical map. What does it look like? I am going to suggest that our map, our Christian story, has a very specific beginning and ending, and if we get those details fixed in our mind—if we keep our story straight—what falls in between makes more sense and gives our mission as members of God's kingdom both clarity and purpose.

Please don't assume that I am not aware of the nuances and details that shape our faith journey. Many of these smaller details are essential to us, but for now let us live in the world of generalities so that we can see these more delicate points in their proper context.

How does our story begin? Move to Genesis, chapters 1 and 2, and the curtain rises on a picture of paradise right here on earth: seas teaming with fish, lands overrun by lush vegetation, human beings shaped in the image of our Creator. A world built in six days, all given life and breath by the invigorating spirit of the Almighty, living by the principle of sabbatical relief. A place where all are given their place and in which humanity shares the responsibility of stewarding the fruits of God's creation.

From this first creation story, we can glean two important facts. First, we are free creatures—God has given to us all the beauty of creation. One must argue that from God's deep sense of delight and love, God has given us this land in a manner that reflects not simply God's love, but also God's justice. As I mentioned in the previous chapter, creation moves and works, breathes and grows over six days. On the seventh it rests—even God has to take a break. Our story begins with the assumption that everything must rest. No one—no object, animal, or plant—can be exploited endlessly. Even God must rest. All parts of creation must have their fair share of rest and, by extension, their portion of all the beauty that is Earth. Justice is the foundation on which our story begins.

The second point we can glean from our beginning: life is a cooperative venture. God does not set human beings into creation hoping they will sit on their hands and do nothing but pray or sleep. God doesn't hand us the remote and say, "Veg out! Have a nice rest." We are to exercise dominion, along with our Creator, over this earth. We're "on call," so to speak, from the beginning. Our role on earth is to be *co-participants* in the unfolding of God's creativity. This beautiful, good earth is our home and God expects us to be great stewards, to participate with God in the nurturing of this great gift.

So, our story begins with justice and co-creation.

These two dimensions are repeated in the second story of creation as found in Genesis 2 beginning in verse 4: the story of Adam and Eve. Again, we find ourselves in a garden of impossible beauty. The love of God is made manifest in every tree and bud, every fruit and flower. In this story, human beings are created as cooperators, not only with God, but also among themselves. We are not singular. We are created in a duality, a community. Before we start our work to assist God with the garden, we turn the "me" into "us." The Garden of Eden is like heaven on earth, a place where communion with God is absolutely transparent. God is next to us.

That's how we begin.

If we turn to the ending of the Bible, and our story, we discover in Revelation 21 and 22 a very similar set of themes.

Leaving aside the bloody details of the book of Revelation, we discover that the writer of the last book of the Bible concludes his vision with an image of a new world descending: "I saw a new heaven and a new earth and the holy city, descending . . . ." Notice this new realm, this heaven-sent beautiful garden of a city, is coming back down to earth. Tears are wiped away, war is gone, fear a distant memory. Justice rules. We begin here on earth in Genesis and it appears that we're never to leave this realm. Our journey ends here too. No flights of fantasy to get our souls into heaven, no skyward, longing glances. Heaven comes down *here* to Earth. Heaven, the realm where God's will rules, does not stay above and beyond human history—but our journey ends when that heaven comes to Earth; a vision that portrays a world in which God's will reigns. The kingdom we have been expecting. We end the good news by establishing it again, here and now.

The Bible begins with a garden where God's will is absolute, and that is exactly where it ends. Our story starts in a place where justice is built right into the hard drive of creation, so to speak, and that is exactly where we end. Another way to say this is to proclaim that our story begins and ends with an affirmation of who we are: "We are a blessing."

Now, I know you will tell me that I have not filled in the very large and ponderous blank that lies between Genesis 3 and Revelation 20. A blank we call "sin." As soon as we reach the third chapter of Genesis, humans start to act out and rebel against their Maker. We fall prey to our fear of mortality. We start asking ourselves, "How I can keep what I have and get what is yours?" We slide into violence, slurs, and slanders that lead to genocides, fratricides, misogyny, and general misery. The Bible is terribly honest about the dark side of human life—and in our liturgical calendar, Lent is often the time when we ring the chimes on the very deadly nature of our sin. The first twenty chapters of Revelation are a grim testimony to the anger and hopelessness of even the best believers and saints among us.

But that is absolutely not how our story begins *or* ends.

How you begin and end the story *does* shape it. Of course, if you begin our journey at chapter three of Genesis, then we will naturally see the Christian religion as salvation history in which human beings are essentially hopeless, failed, and frail. We will always need rescuing. In that case, our story would be always be about what we are not. We are not, and never will be, good enough. So, we need Jesus as our savior: the one who extends a hand down into the gutter of our sin and pulls us out of the mire. How many hymns have stated just that?

If you begin our story at Genesis 3, Jesus is God's lifesaver for a drowning experiment. We are a failing enterprise and the only way we can ever hope to survive is for God and Jesus to make a deal in heaven (what theologians call "substitutionary" atonement), and save us from ourselves. Our Easter-oriented story is shaped by our failure, as a species, and our need for salvation.

But if we start our story at the beginning, as the Bible's authors surely intended, then our map is not shaped by what we are not, but what we *are*. Sure, everyone needs salvation, but that's not the first or last word. Our story begins and ends as an invitation for our participation in God's plan for creation: justice and love. We are not placed here on earth as lost creatures, all hoping to escape to heaven. Luke's story of Simon's dinner party reinforces this message. The ones who think they are broken, failed, and rejected are actually saved and blessed.

We are given life, today, so that we can work with God to make this earth right, to shape it into the heaven sent down to earth described in Revelation. And when the company of Jesus concluded their prayer, they were invoking this kingdom into being: not as theory or a spiritual condition, but as reigning reality in which everything is changed: right down to table etiquette.

Amen.

10

Consequences of Living Our Prayers: Always Trust Your Heart

The Key Question

"So what?"

Have I done my job? Every good book inspires the reader to ask, "So what?" Are there any concrete daily steps that flow from these theological precepts? If we understand the material in the previous chapters and accept it as reasonable, then what does it mean for us? That's the key question.

Let us agree that the early disciples established a new world when they gathered. Quite literally, they prayed the kingdom of God into life. The Prayer was both a reminder and a convocation of a people on "the Way." Not fanciful or futuristic, this realm was an agreed-upon reality by which they governed their lives. They had their positive alternative kingdom that was lived in opposition to the Roman Empire. How could that possibly help us who live within the shadow of the American Empire?

On one level, the answer to the question of consequences is very straightforward: Our role is to do the same. Let's pray God's kingdom into being. Just because some 2,000 years separate us from the original disciples, there is no diminishment of vision. God's realm is waiting to be established here again among us.

In fact, we may be in a more favorable position to undertake this task than past generations. After the initial generations of believers passed on, the church accommodated itself to values of the Roman Empire. It took several centuries, but eventually it became the "official" religion. Under Constantine, "the Way" became "the church" and suffered considerable domestication in that transition. It was turned into an institution with prescribed prayers and practices, designed to acculturate believers to the principles of empire.

When Christianity was turned into the "authorized" spiritual tradition, it was recruited into the ranks of those who proclaimed imperial theology: Peace through war and violence. In consequence, we adjusted our sense of justice, telling ourselves it was necessary to accept the practicality of going with half-measures and accommodations to economic necessities. We toned down the prophetic voices of the Scriptures and gave spiritual interpretations to the more strident social justice passages.

The first community of pilgrims were soon replaced by those who wanted to transform the kingdom of God's healing circle of equals into a pyramid of spiritual patronage. In this latter case, priests assigned relative virtue to those deemed to be "righteous" and excluded the others as unworthy. The early community that shared daily bread and justice was transformed over generations of accommodation to empire, into a church that was seduced by the values and allures of imperial power. Eventually, its ministry and mission went along willingly with what one might call the imprisonment of its "prophetic imagination."[1]

Fortunately, the Constantinian exile of the church appears to be over. In the past fifty years, the Northern American church has been thrown out of the social clubs of status and the corridors of power. We're no longer consulted on social programming or foreign policy. It is not necessary to be a devout believer to even be considered for positions of influence in the caucus room or corporate office. In fact, it might be considered a liability to actually have faith in a vision other than the reigning wisdom of consumerism and constant growth.

So, what do we do?

I would suggest three steps: First, let us open our eyes. God's reign is present still, we just have to look harder to find it. Second, we could get started by living out some of the principles of the Prayer: free bread, forgiven loans. They worked before, why not again? Finally, there is a spiritual challenge: We have to trust our heart. Let's look at each of these as a conclusion to our study.

1. Brueggemann, *The Prophetic Imagination*.

Believing is Seeing

I have seen the kingdom of God often. The more I expect to see it, the more evident it becomes. Flashes of a new world breaking into this one. Two moments stand out for me: one a momentary sparkle of God's reign, the second a longer, more lasting picture.

Twenty years ago, I was working in a church where we sponsored a self-help group on welfare rights. People who lived on fixed incomes had precious little financial security and even less spiritual assurance. The church gave them a place to meet and the courage to exercise their own voices in their defense. We had roundtable discussions with government ministers, we marched in protests, joined in hunger strikes, served coffee to the line-ups at the local charity office, and cooked meals together.

This last activity was intended as a community-builder. As the group was run by people on welfare, they knew from firsthand experience that at the third week in the month, the food budget was spent and the cupboard was bare. What irony; poor people in this wealthy country spend the last week of the month eating potatoes and peanut butter, or going to the soup kitchen. We planned our meals to coincide with this difficult time. The deal was quite simple: the church paid for the food, the group prepared and served it. We planned big meals like turkey or ham with all the fixings. The first night we planned for thirty people, and sixty-five came. It turned out to be a great hit.

I would tell the leaders of the group to work the crowd while I'd take care of the kitchen, washing the dishes and serving platters. To accomplish my part, I would recruit members of the church. I had an additional motive in assigning the tasks in that way: Not only did it put the folks on income assistance in a position of leadership, it also invited people from higher levels of society into a serving role. A reversal of power that would be instructive to everyone.

I recall one night in that kitchen, I had persuaded the province's chief neurosurgeon to help with washing pots. Brian was always willing. A very sensitive man with a great heart, he was eager to help when he was free. So, he had his hands in the dirty water scrubbing potato scum off the rim of the large boiling pot. Beside him was John, an unemployed cook. John was part of the group, but he wanted to work the kitchen. So, there he was talking to Brian. I could think of no greater contrast in social standing and economic power than these two men with their hands in the same dishwater. There they were laughing and telling jokes, exchanging commentary on hockey teams and arguing over city politics. God's reign was present in that encounter.

It was fleeting, but in the leveling of power I could understand why the first "kingdom of God" gathering had such power. When accepted, social barriers are broken down—who knows what good will and generosity can flow in all directions! The stereotypes and prejudices that have kept us apart are gone, and suddenly the healing of shared compassion can happen.

Surely if we wonder what we should do with what we have learned from the Prayer community, it is to recreate this kind of equality of relationship: a share-circle where food is freely given. Can we imagine such a community *not* based on pity or charitable benevolence, but a mutual effort in pursuit of a common cause?

My second glimpse of the kingdom is more detailed. It involves the question of same-sex marriage.

Several years ago, the Canadian parliament made it possible for people of the same sex to enjoy the fruits and responsibilities of legal matrimony. Throughout Canada, churches were then asked if they would perform same-sex marriages. Some denominations refused to participate, which was their right, of course. Others, like the United Church of Canada, left the decision to local congregations.

In the church where I served, the wisdom of the leadership was that we not take a vote or push people into taking a position on this question. They argued quite persuasively that after studying the issue and giving considerable room for people to express their opinion, we would follow our prescribed practice: to weigh each request for marriage on its own merits—be they a heterosexual or homosexual couple.

This turned out to be very good counsel. I was aware of several members of the church for whom any consideration of same-sex marriage was an offense to their faith. I visited with them and laid out what I believed to be the best arguments on both sides. We agreed to disagree, and then we had coffee. Community can survive in the midst of diversity of views.

When a lesbian couple approached our church and asked for permission to be married in the sanctuary, there was no question. Not a word of debate. You see, one member of the couple had an extensive theological background, working on a PhD in Hebrew Scripture. She had been writing our church school curriculum and working with our kids for a few years. Everyone loved and respected her. Her partner was a local doctor and had a strong reputation for compassion in town. Who could possibly object to these two women getting married? We had watched their love flourish in the church. There was nothing but applause to greet their request.

Wedding plans moved forward, but it turned out that the reception hall was unavailable. So, the couple came back to the church and asked if they could pay the women's auxiliary to serve the reception in the church gym. That usually is not a problem. However, I knew there were five women for whom this kind of marriage was a serious problem. I went to see each one and they again voiced their dissent, but they also said they would help as it was "their duty." More coffee!

But there was one setback. The couple asked the church if they could serve wine at their wedding. The church board refused; it was a long-standing policy that there was to be no liquor sold or served on the premises. Oh well, we can't ask for everything all at once.

The plans went ahead and as the big day arrived, I saw more energy around the building. The janitor was working at polishing anything that didn't move. The kitchen and gym were scrubbed. You could have eaten off of the floor when the women's group was done scouring the rooms even remotely connected with the wedding.

It was the custom of the women's group to sit at the back of the sanctuary when they served a reception. As I looked to the back, there they were, listening and leaning forward. Even the five women who had trouble with this ceremony were present. I could see smiles and sympathy all round. The ceremony was delightful, creative and very classy, including children and elders with equal dignity.

When we got down to the gym, it was decked out in balloons and streamers. The tables were perfectly laid out, and we were all ready for a good dance. Then, as we were seated, and before the food was brought out, a couple of the women—one of whom was dead set against same-sex marriage—came out from the kitchen looked furtively about, and then quickly poured wine into the juice glasses at the brides' table and others round about them. I heard one of them whisper to the happy couple, "You can't have a wedding reception without wine. Silly church rules be damned!"

It was at that moment that I knew the kingdom of God was present and always possible. It comes in spite of our best intentions to keep it out. It overrides our practical and reasonable objections. God's reign does not wait for permission, and takes no account of propriety or property. Amen!

It has been my experience that the more I look for the kingdom of God and expect it, the more often I see it. There are the very generous acts of compassion: food taken regularly to the hungry, hours spent visiting the lost, etc. It's there in your community of faith, you simply have to name it. When we reach beyond the expected response, when we move with passion to restore just relations, God is ruling our lives. I would invite you to look carefully around you. As Jesus said to his disciples, the kingdom of God is already present.

Getting Started

In the time of Jesus, the first step to living into God's reign was to make and share bread. Perhaps that can also be our second response to the Prayer. I mentioned "Bread Day" in the chapter on Daily Bread. It was not initially our intention to live out the Prayer. When we began the bread-making project, we simply wanted to give food to hungry people; to be a surprising presence of delight and gratitude in the center of the city. No one turns down fresh bread. It seemed like a natural entry. We took bread to offices round the church and hoped to engender great community. We had no idea how this simple act would begin to establish the basis for hope. People began to anticipate "Bread Day." They'd start to joke about it, ask church members when the next one was coming so they wouldn't miss it.

Whatever the church has lost, we have retained the importance of food. We know that, in shared meals, healing takes place. So, I would invite communities of faith to live their daily bread. Start giving away fresh loaves, cakes, cookies, whatever you can bake. Don't use food for fundraising. There is much greater benefit in giving it away. What would happen if we became the people who were recognized by our free bread?

I recall how Bob, a ministry colleague, was once invited into the country for a funeral of a close friend. He had a vague idea of where the chapel at the crossroads was to be found, but when he got close, all the roads seemed to lead in the wrong direction. Bob took at least two wrong turns and knew that he was completely lost. There was no white chapel in sight. Even though he knew he had to be close, there was no street sign to point him in the right direction.

As Bob watched the car's digital clock tick closer to the time the funeral was to start, he got frantic. Ahead on the right was an old farmhouse, so he decided to ask for directions. However, before he could turn down the lane, a couple appeared at the kitchen door. They were well-dressed and obviously leaving. In their hands were two large plates of sandwiches and

Bob told himself, "Just follow the plate of sandwiches and you'll find the church." So, he did. The couple guided him down a couple of well-rutted lanes and, sure enough, they all arrived at the small chapel. The funeral was now ready to begin. Bob told me later, "If you want to find Christians, just follow the food." May that be written above all the doors of our buildings.

It seems too easy, but let me promise you that when you start on this journey of giving food away, who knows where it will take you? Don't expect to be unchanged. If we keep our eyes open and look carefully into the eyes of those we serve, who knows what they will say and where they will take us? It will not be long before we have to learn the grace of being served. For those we offer free food will quite naturally want to return the favor.

It doesn't have to be free bread. There are endless examples of living out the principles behind the forgiveness of loans: micro-economic projects, mission trips to disaster zones, small loans enterprises, fair trade enterprises. Google "economic justice" or "fair trade" and you will have an endless stream of ideas.

The real work in this second step is having the courage to get started. It is easier to complain about the darkness than to open the doors, let in the light, and take a chance. I know this. There is no quick answer to our fears. We have to face them, recognizing that we are not alone and that the one who shaped us from the beginning will not desert us when we begin to act on it.

Always Trust Your Heart

Allow me to be frank as we conclude. If you have followed the logic of this text to this point, then perhaps I can presume on your goodwill to speak bluntly. I recognize myself in the following caricature of the church. So, this is not a blast so much as a confession.

Here's our problem: We don't really *believe* it.

We don't believe our story or its power. We may have courage to be generous and compassionate. Indeed, we may feel a great need to make a difference in God's world, but we lack conviction. It is as if what I have just described as a possible reign of God that commands our loyalty is "just a movie." A very interesting bit of film, but not real life.

Have we told ourselves too often that things can't change? That we are an institution that is dying; that the Jesus story is quaint and sometimes comforting, but not really a road map for life or for creating community? "No one cares anymore, particularly young people."

Or perhaps we have all we need and we don't really want more. After all, first-world Christians have it pretty well. They can believe in Jesus, like a good hobby: something that takes up our time, gives us pleasure, but isn't "real life." So, we offer some of our excess to those in need, but we never expect our church or our faith to radically change us. It's not in the cards. It's not that we're cynical or apathetic; we just believe that the Jesus miracles of bread can't happen for us. Nevertheless, even while first-world Christians have constructed their lives so they have all they need, there is one thing we lack: true belief.

In the final analysis, the Prayer is a world-transforming event. It invites believers into a new world view. Can we enter into it and truly believe? This is perhaps the most challenging dimension of our current spiritual context. It seems a bit "cheesy" or "impractical" to have fervent belief. No one expects God to actually work with us to change the world. That's too silly.

Our challenge is essentially spiritual. We don't trust our hearts. We have told ourselves too often that it can't be possible to believe so much that the world changes, that mountains move, or justice comes to stay. We tell our hearts not to hope, that things will never improve. So, we don't attempt it—and this is precisely our problem as a community of faith.

And here I conclude for there are no easy steps to restore or inspire true believing. The history of the Christian movement is littered with evidence that God's reign can come alive and be a vital agent for transforming the world: the emancipation of slaves, the ongoing confrontations with racism and sexism, the care of the sick, and the comfort of the lost. While these great transformations began in widely different contexts and circumstances, they all have one thing in common: people believed they would change the world, with God's help of course.

Now, it's your turn. Do you really trust your heart?

Bibliography

Apostolides, S. "Our Lord's Prayer in one hundred different languages." London: W. M. Watts, 1869.

Augustine of Hippo. *The Confessions of St. Augustine*. London: J. M. Dent & Sons, 1945.

Bonhoeffer, Dietrich. *Letters and Papers from Prison*. Edited by E. Bethge. London: SCM, 1953.

Borg, Marcus, and John Dominic Crossan. *The First Paul: Reclaiming the Radical Visionary Behind the Church's Conservative Icon*. San Francisco: Harper Collins, 2009.

Brueggemann, Walter. *The Prophet Imagination*. Philadelphia: Fortress, 1978.

Crossan, John Dominic, and Jonathan Reed. *Excavating Jesus: Beneath the Stones, Behind the Texts*. New York: Harper San Francisco, 2002.

Crossan, John Dominic. *God and Empire*. New York: HarperOne, 2007.

———. *The Greatest Prayer*. New York: HarperOne, 2010.

Fox, Matthew. *The Reinvention of Work: A New Vision of Livelihood for Our Time*. New York: Harper Collins, 1995.

Hall, Douglas J. *When You Pray*. Valley Forge, PA: Judson, 1987.

Mayes, Frances. *Bella Tuscany: The Sweet Life in Italy*. New York: Broadway, 1999.

Miller, Robert, ed. *The Complete Gospels*. Santa Rosa, CA: Polebridge, 1994.

APPENDIX

Translations and Versions
of the Lord's Prayer

List of texts:

1. New International Version

2. King James Version

3. New Living Translation

4. Scholar's Versions:
   - Matthew
   - Luke

5. Vulgate (Latin)

6. Classical Greek

7. English Translation of Spanish Service in Luyano, Cuba

1. New International Version

"Our Father in heaven,
hallowed be your name,
your kingdom come,
your will be done,
on earth as it is in heaven.
Give us today our daily bread.
And forgive us our debts,
as we also have forgiven our debtors.
And lead us not into temptation,
but deliver us from the evil one." (Matt 6:9–13)

2. King James Version

"Our Father which art in heaven,
Hallowed be thy name.
Thy kingdom come, Thy will be done in earth, as it is in heaven.
Give us this day our daily bread.
And forgive us our debts, as we forgive our debtors.
And lead us not into temptation, but deliver us from evil: For thine is the
kingdom, and the power, and the glory, for ever. Amen." (Matt 6:9–13)

3. New Living Translation

"Our Father in heaven,
may your name be kept holy.
May your kingdom come soon.
May your will be done on earth,
as it is in heaven.
Give us today the food we need,
and forgive us our sins,
as we have forgiven those who sin against us.
And don't let us yield to temptation,
but rescue us from the evil one." (Matt 6:9–13)

4. Scholar's Versions

Matthew

Our Father in heaven,
Your name is revered,
Impose your imperial rule,
Enact your will on earth as you have in heaven.
Provide us with the bread we need for the day,
Forgive our debts to the extent we have forgiven those in debt to us.
And please don't subject us to test after test,
But rescue us from the evil one."

Luke

"Father, your name be revered,
Impose your imperial rule,
Provide us with the bread we need day by day,
Forgive our sins since we forgive everyone in debt to us,
And please don't subject us to test after test."

5. Vulgate

"*Pater noster qui in caelis es sanctificetur nomen tuum*
veniat regnum tuum fiat voluntas tua sicut in caelo et in terra
panem nostrum supersubstantialem da nobis hodie
et dimitte nobis debita nostra sicut et nos dimisimus debitoribus nostris
et ne inducas nos in temptationem sed libera nos a malo" (*Matthaeus* 6:9–13)

6. Classical Greek

Πάτερ ἡμῶν ὁ ἐν τοῖς οὐρανοῖς,
ἁγιασθήτω τὸ ὄνομάσου,
ἐλθέτω ἡ βασιλεία σου,
γενηθήτω τὸ θέλημά σου,
ὡς ἐν οὐρανῷ καὶ ἐπὶ τῆς γῆς

155

τὸν ἄρτον ἡμῶν τὸν ἐπιούσιον δὸς ἡμῖν σήμερον,

καὶ ἄφες ἡμῖν τὰ ὀφειλήματα ἡμῶν,

ὡς καὶ ἡμεῖς ἀφίεμεν τοῖς ὀφειλέταις ἡμῶν

καὶ μὴ εἰσενέγκῃς ἡμᾶς εἰς πειρασμόν

ἀλλὰ ῥῦσαι ἡμᾶς ἀπὸ τοῦ πονηροῦ.

Ὅτι σοῦ ἐστὶν ἡ βασιλεία καὶ ἡ δόξα εἰς τοὺς αἰῶνας.

Ἀμήν.[1]

7. English Translation of Spanish Service in Luyano, Cuba

"Our Father

You who lives in all those who love truth

Make your reign which you have given

Come to our heart

And the love of which your son gave, that love which lives in us

Give us the bread of unity

Christ[,] give us your peace and forget our weakness

As we forget that of others

Don't let us fall into temptation of God for the pity of the world. Amen.

Another version is used in Luyano Reformed Presbyterian Church (sung to "House of the Rising Sun"). This version is used by other denominations in Cuba as well. The following is a Spanish text with English interlinear translation:

Padre nuestro tú eres que estás

Our Father, you are the one who lives

En los que aman la verdad

In those who love the truth

Haz que el Reino que por ti se dio

Make the Reign which was given for you

Llegue pronto a nuestro corazón

Come quickly in our hearts.

Y el amor que tu Hijo nos dejó, el amor

And the love which your Son gave to us, that love

Esté ya con nosotros

1. Apostolides, "Our Lord's Prayer in one hundred different languages."

Is still with us.
Y en el pan de la unidad
And in the bread of unity
Cristo danos tú la paz
Christ gives us peace.
Y olvídate de nuestro mal
And forget our faults
Si olvidamos de los demás
As we forget those of others
No permitas que caigamos en tentación
Do not let us fall into temptation
Oh Señor
And Lord
Y ten piedad del mundo
Have pity on the world
Y ten piedad del mundo
Have pity on the world.

CPSIA information can be obtained
at www.ICGtesting.com
Printed in the USA
LVHW09s0306201018
594219LV00001B/51/P

9 781532 618154